SOUP!

SOUP!

Vava Berry

PHOTOGRAPHY BY YUKI SUGIURA

PAVILION

contents

introduction

Soup is the ultimate comfort food. We all have childhood memories of soup. When I was growing up in France, soup and cheese was the ritual evening meal for my grandparents. When they said to their friends '*Venez manger la soupe*' ('Come eat the soup'), they meant 'come for dinner'. The soup plate would never leave the table. We would wipe it clean with a piece of bread, turn it over, and eat the cheese off the upside-down plate.

Some kids wake up to the smell of coffee; for me, it was onions and leeks slowly cooking or oxtail gently bubbling from very early morning. One of my best memories is of the famous *soupe à l'oignon gratinée* a friend cooked for me years ago. She prepared it with three different types of onions that she forgot over a low heat for one hour. The stock she added had been simmering for five hours. She toasted bread slices in the fireplace before covering them with cheese. The cheese became bubbly and golden under the grill. The slight smoky taste of the bread added another dimension to this amazing soup. It was heaven!

Every country has a soup tradition. In China, a clear soup accompanies the meal like a beverage. In Vietnam, *Pho*, a beef and noodle soup, is served for breakfast. In Morocco, *Harira*, a nutritious mix of lamb, lentils, chickpeas, garlic, herbs and spices is served every evening to break the fast of Ramadan. Although nicknamed 'Jewish penicillin', many cultures have adopted chicken soup as a cure for the common cold.

Soup also means the end of waste in your kitchen. Any leftovers can be added to a soup to create a more nutritious combination, enhance tastes or add texture. Some of the recipes will give you hints and ideas on how to do just that.

The soups in this book are classified by needs, moods and occasions rather than ingredients. You can create a whole dinner party around one soup, cook a healthy lunch that will make your colleagues jealous, be creative for very little money, play chef for the night, bring a soup to the table within ten minutes, and get your summer picnic sorted.

I hope these recipes will inspire you, and above all make your life easier!

Vava

Q and A

What is the secret of a good soup?
The stock, of course! I have basic recipes at the end of the book for stocks. You will notice that I have three different recipes for vegetable stocks to avoid all your vegetarian soups tasting the same. Sometimes I use the vegetable peels and trimmings of the soup ingredients to make stocks. It should give you that nice feeling of not wasting anything. It also gives the stock its own identity.

Stocks take time to make. Whenever I buy meat, I ask the butcher for bones and freeze them. When I have enough bones, I make a stock. The same goes for leftover carcasses, roast bones or ham trimmings – they can all be chucked in the same pan. Fish stocks are also very economical to make. Most fishmongers will give you fish heads and bones for free. However, be careful not to overcook fish stock, as it will lose its fresh fish flavour. You can also find traditional Japanese fish and vegetable stocks in the miso soup recipes (pp.19, 67 and 112).

What's the difference between a soup and a potage?
In Medieval England, *soup* was the name given to a flavoured broth mixed with a few 'sops' of bread. In France, it was the name given to the slice of bread used as a plate to hold a stew. Later, the slice of bread was placed in a soup plate and covered with broth. By extension it became the general term for an evening meal. The term *potage* appeared in the 13th century to describe food cooked in a pot and, by extension, an upgrade from broth and bread. It is still used as a smarter name to describe a soup. Then you get into many fancy names: a *consommé* is a clear meat broth, a *velouté* is a creamy or thickened soup and a *bisque* is a puréed shellfish soup.

Why do you give different serving proportions throughout the book?
A serving for a starter is about 350 ml/12 fl oz/1½ cups. Some soups are more filling and would be about 250 ml/8 fl oz/1 cup. You eat less of a cold soup, so portions are also smaller: I allow about 250 ml/8 fl oz/1 cup. And what I call a tapas portion is about 100 ml/3½ oz/scant ½ cup.

Can you really make a soup in 15 minutes?
This is a challenge – you usually need time to make a soup, so I have found ways of boosting the flavours. My favourite one is Cream of rocket and goat's milk (p.26) – it is ultra simple, takes 10 minutes and has an amazing flavour. This section is ideal for those who are convinced they cannot cook. The recipes are so easy to follow that I hope their fear of cooking will disappear!

What do you think of ready-made stocks and cubes?
These are very practical and I have used them to boost flavours in the Instant Magic section. I prefer organic low sodium stock cubes. You can improve a stock cube by simmering it with leftover chicken carcasses, vegetable trimmings or herbs.

Can you make a soup with virtually anything?
Sometimes the best soups are made using leftovers from the fridge. So yes, you can. Just remember that too many ingredients in a soup can be as disastrous as too many chefs in the kitchen. Whatever you do, the quality of the ingredients you use is crucial. This is true for cooking in general but even more obvious in soups, where ingredients are diluted. One day I bought carrots in a hurry from a little grocery store on my way home. The soup I made from these carrots was very bland. I had to buy another batch of carrots to test it again and it was fine. If you use tasteless ingredients, your soup will be tasteless.

How would you know you bought tasteless carrots?
It's hard to munch on a carrot in a store and decide whether you are going to buy it or not. The intensity of the colour, unblemished skin, and the smell are good indications of the quality. Weight is also a sign of quality. Cauliflower and cabbages should feel heavy and full. Courgettes should be shiny. Onion and garlic bulbs should be very firm to the touch.

You often fry or bake ingredients prior to simmering. Is this important?

If you place a mixture of cubed vegetables in a saucepan and cook them with water, or if you sweat the same mixture in a bit of oil for 10 minutes, and then cook them in water, the results will be dramatically different. It is interesting to try it to really understand the process. Sweating or roasting ingredients first really draws out the flavours. You will also notice that I add salt while sweating vegetables or baking meat; this also helps to concentrate flavours and you will need less salt in your soup.

Why a whole section on chilled soups?

Chilled soups make fabulous summer starters. They are also perfect for picnics. I really like them as little *tapas* before meals or as palate cleansers between courses. For warm soup fanatics, some of these chilled soups are quite delicious heated up.

Are soups that healthy? Don't you lose nutrients after such long cooking?

On the contrary, all the nutrients go straight into the stock. Soups are a good way to diet, as long as you control the amount of salt you put in them. Eating soups will give you a varied low fat diet and a good intake of liquid.

Speaking of salt, what can you do if a soup is too salty?

If you taste your soup often and readjust the seasoning as you are cooking, it should not be too salty. Remember to drink a bit of water before you taste. You can easily impair your judgment if you don't clean your taste buds.

If you really have gone wrong, you can add big chunks of raw potato and cook the soup for an extra 20 minutes. The potatoes will absorb some of the salt from the stock. The bigger the chunks, the easier they will be to remove. If you have dropped the salt shaker into the soup, there is not a lot you can do.

What is the best way to blend a soup?

A handheld blender works really well, while a blender will give a smoother texture. My favourite blender doesn't need electricity — it is the old-fashioned food mill, or *mouli*. You will notice that I often pass the soups through a sieve for a smoother texture. Fibres from leek and celery or bean skins get caught in the grids of a food mill. It will blend and sieve the soup at the same time. The only drawback is the extra elbow grease needed.

What is your favourite memory of soup?

Once we were driving to Paris from London when the most violent storm broke — you couldn't see more than two metres ahead. It was getting late and so we decided to stop overnight. We were lucky to find a hotel with a restaurant quickly. That evening they served the most amazing chestnut soup. I kept thinking of that chestnut soup throughout the rest of the meal. After dessert when the waiter cleared the table and asked if we wanted anything else, implying coffee or tea, I asked for a second portion of the chestnut soup. The chef was thrilled.

Do you know any soup jokes?

It's a quote from the movie *Dumb and Dumber*:
Lloyd: What's the *soup du jour*?
Waitress: It's the soup of the day.
Lloyd: Mmm... that sounds good, I'll have that.

instant magic

This really is the magical section of this book: hot soups that can be cooked in less than 20 minutes and still be delicious!

Fast cooking is about taking shortcuts. Peas, for example, are the miracle fast food. They can be whizzed up in no time. Sweetcorn, scallops, rainbow trout or smoked haddock also take little time to cook, and can be stocked in the freezer for those times when your fridge looks depressingly empty.

I don't usually like cooking with tinned food, but I am really impressed by the quality of Spanish tinned products like piquillo peppers and chickpeas, and certain Italian brands of tinned tomatoes. I have relied heavily on tinned food in this section: passata, coconut milk and evaporated milk give you a good base for speeding up soup-making. All you need is to add a few fresh ingredients. Some of the recipes are perfect for when moving house or camping.

But the best part of this chapter is the ultra-simplicity of some of the recipes, like pea, wasabi and dill soup, or Thai rainbow trout with coconut. Even if you have hardly touched a saucepan in your life before, everyone will think you are an amazing cook!

Tomato, coconut & peanut soup

Serves 4
Preparation: 5 minutes
Cooking time: 18 minutes

This is cupboard cooking at its best. You can add wilted spinach or chard for a green touch, but the soup is delicious on its own. Kids love it mixed with cooked orzo pasta or mini macaroni. The coconut milk and peanut butter make it rich and nourishing, so portions should be smaller than with other soups.

ingredients

600 ml/1 pint /2½ cups tomato passata
2 tsp sugar
1 pinch saffron
1 x 400 ml/14 fl oz tin reduced-fat coconut milk
2 tsp soy sauce
4–5 tbsp peanut butter (with no added sugar)
2 tsp olive oil
100 g /3½ oz/generous 1 cup baby spinach or chard, washed

Hot sauce, such as Tabasco, to serve

method

Place the passata in a 2-litre soup pan. Add 200 ml/7 fl oz/generous ¾ cup of water, and the sugar and saffron. Bring to a boil, reduce the heat and simmer for 10 minutes.

Add the coconut milk and soy sauce. Simmer for 2–3 minutes, stirring constantly or the coconut will curdle. Add the peanut butter and leave to simmer for another minute.

Meanwhile, heat the olive oil in a large frying pan and quickly stir-fry the spinach or chard until just wilted.

Serve the soup with the wilted spinach or chard, and let each guest season it with hot sauce.

tip

Use reduced-fat coconut milk in soups – it's healthier and will give a lighter consistency to your soup.

66 Take a fresh look in your kitchen cupboard – it may contain wonders. 99

Pea, wasabi & dill soup

Serves 4
Preparation: 2 minutes
Cooking time: 10 minutes

Wasabi is a small leafy root originating from Japan. It is often called 'Japanese horseradish' for its similar taste, but is actually from the watercress family. Wasabi is delicate and expensive to grow. Most of the wasabi sold in Europe is a substitute for wasabi, a root similar to horseradish that is ironically called '*seiyou wasabi*' ('Western wasabi'). It is grated and coloured green. It is the ingredient I have used in this soup. I have never tasted real freshly grated wasabi, but I would probably not use it in a soup. By the way, horseradish also works well in this soup.

ingredients

2 organic vegetable or
chicken stock cubes
800 g / 1¾ lb frozen petit pois (baby
peas)
3–5 tsp wasabi paste
1 tbsp fresh dill, chopped
Salt and pepper

method

Bring 1 litre/1¾ pints of water to a boil in a 2-litre soup pan. Add the stock cubes and stir until dissolved. Add the frozen peas. Bring to a boil, reduce the heat, and simmer for 5 minutes. Remove from the heat and leave to cool for 10 minutes.

Place half of the soup in a blender and process until smooth. Pour into the saucepan. Repeat with the other half.

In a separate bowl, mix the wasabi with some of the pea soup to dilute. Start with 3 teaspoons of wasabi, then add some more if you like it stronger. Adjust the seasoning, gently reheat the soup, and serve.

tip

The tender skin of petit pois blends well. If you still want a very fine, smooth texture, pass the soup through a fine sieve, then season it with dill and wasabi.

Asparagus & radish top soup

Serves 4
Preparation: 5 minutes
Cooking time: 15 minutes

Radish tops add a wonderful taste to soups. Like watercress, it is best to incorporate them at the end. Overcooking them will waste their delicate, peppery flavour. You can replace the radish tops by a mixture of watercress and rocket. I'm not a great fan of instant mashed potatoes, but when I was trying different thickeners for soups, I was impressed by the result here.

ingredients
500 g/1 lb 2 oz green asparagus
2 tbsp olive oil
1 onion, finely chopped
Salt and pepper
30 g/1 oz/1⅛ cup instant mashed potatoes
200 g/7 oz radish tops, washed and roughly chopped

to serve
100 g/3½ oz fresh goat's cheese
20 g/¾ oz/⅓ cup fresh coriander (cilantro)

method
Trim off the woody end of the asparagus. Cut the rest into 2.5 cm/1 in pieces.

Heat the oil in a 3-litre soup pan and fry the onion and asparagus together over a medium heat for 2 minutes, until the onions are soft and the asparagus bright green and fragrant. Season well with salt and freshly ground black pepper. Add the instant mash powder, then 1 litre/1¾ pints of water. Simmer for 10 minutes.

Mash the goat's cheese and coriander together with a fork until well blended.

Add the radish tops to the soup and simmer for 2 more minutes. Turn off the heat and leave to cool for 10 minutes.

Whiz the soup in the blender in 3 batches, or roughly whiz with a hand-held electric blender. Return to the pan and heat up gently. Serve the soup garnished with a generous tablespoon of the goat's cheese and coriander mixture.

Cream of corn with crab

Serves 4
Preparation: 5 minutes
Cooking time: 15 minutes

I discovered evaporated milk while working on this book. It is lighter than cream but not as filling, and it gives a beautiful creamy consistency to soups. This soup has quite a kick, so use only half of a jalapeño chilli if you are sensitive to hot dishes.

ingredients

2 tbsp olive oil
1 bunch spring onions (scallions), washed and finely sliced
1 garlic clove, crushed
500 g/1 lb 2 oz frozen corn kernels
1 fresh green jalapeño chilli, deseeded and finely chopped
1 pinch saffron
1 x 410 g tin evaporated milk (400 ml/14 fl oz)
3 tbsp polenta

A freshly cooked crab, to serve

method

Heat the oil in a 3-litre soup pan. Fry the sliced spring onion and garlic for 2 minutes, or until the onion is wilted and the garlic slightly golden. Add the frozen corn kernels and fry for 7 minutes. They will have defrosted by then and might stick to the bottom. Don't worry, a few burnt bits will add more taste, but stir frequently. Add the jalapeño and saffron and stir for 1 more minute.

Add the evaporated milk and, using the tin as a measuring jug, add 1 ½ tins of water. Bring to a boil, sprinkle the polenta on the surface, stir well, and continue to simmer for 5 minutes, stirring from time to time. It is now ready.

This soup can be eaten on its own or with fresh crab meat.

Sopa de tortilla

Serves 4–6
Preparation: 5 minutes
Cooking time: 20 minutes

This is my speedy version of this famous Mexican classic made with leftover tortillas. You still need two ingredients that are not that quick to find: good-quality corn tortillas and chipotle chillies. Some supermarkets sell a chipotle paste, which is quite good. In speciality stores or on the internet, you can also find tinned chipotle chillies 'in adobo' (marinated), which are very hot and quite delicious. Corn tortillas that are sold in supermarkets are too sweet – you are better off ordering them online with your chipotle chillies.

ingredients

1 tbsp sunflower oil
1 small onion, finely sliced
1 garlic clove, crushed
1 x 680 g/1½ lb jar passata with onion and garlic
1 chicken or vegetable stock cube
1–2 tbsp chipotle paste or 2 tinned chipotle chillies
100 ml/3½ fl oz/scant ½ cup sunflower oil, for deep frying
6 x 15 cm/6 in corn tortillas
1 avocado
2 spring onions (scallions)
100 g/3½ oz crumbly cheese (such as Lancashire)

method

Heat the oil in a 3-litre heavy pan. Add the onion slices and fry over medium heat for 3–4 minutes, until soft and slightly coloured. Add the crushed garlic and cook for 30 seconds more. Add the passata, 750 ml/1¼ pints of water, the stock cube and chipotle paste or chillies, and simmer for 15 minutes.

Meanwhile, heat the rest of the oil in a medium-sized frying pan. Cut the tortillas into 5 mm/¼ in strips. Fry in four batches for about 2 minutes, until golden. Drain on a piece of kitchen roll and set aside.

There is an easy way to dice an avocado. Halve the avocado, remove the stone. Holding the avocado half in one hand, make parallel slits with a knife one way then across inside the skin (do not cut the skin, or you will cut your hand). Scoop the little cubes out with a large spoon. Repeat for the other half. Finely slice the spring onion and grate the cheese. These are your garnishes for the soup.

Divide the tortilla strips between 4 or 6 soup plates. Ladle the soup on top, and garnish with spring onion, avocado and cheese. Place the jar of chipotle paste (or leftover chillies) on the table for an extra garnish.

" *This soup is very filling; it will happily serve 6 as an appetizer.* "

Miso soup with scallops & pak choi

Serves 4
Preparation: 5 minutes
Cooking time: 10 minutes

ingredients
8 spring onions (scallions),
finely sliced
200 g/7 oz pak choi (bok choy),
finely chopped
300 g/11 oz scallops, sliced
4 to 5 tbsp *dashi miso* (soy bean
paste with *bonito* extract)
3 g/⅛ oz *wakame* (dried seaweed)

There are many ways of making a miso soup. The proper way involves soaking *kombu*, using *bonito* flakes and miso paste. You will find a recipe in the power lunch section (p.67). In this quick version, I use *dashi miso* paste, which is sold in the refrigerated section of Japanese grocery stores and certain specialist shops and is far superior to the instant powdered miso soup you can get in most supermarkets. The *dashi miso* combines stock, *bonito* and soy bean paste into one paste that is simply diluted in simmering water. It will keep in the fridge for months. *Wakame* is sold dried and will rehydrate when added to the soup. It is high in minerals and vitamins. It is also delicious in salads and rice dishes. Again, both *dashi miso* and *wakame* can be found in Japanese grocery stores and some specialist shops. Scallops are wonderful in miso soup and turn it into a very stylish starter.

method
Bring 1 litre/1¾ pints of water to a simmer in a 3-litre soup pan. Add the spring onions and cook for 1 minute. Add the pak choi, and cook for 3 minutes. Add the slices of scallop and their corals and simmer for 2 more minutes. Add the *dashi miso* and stir until well diluted. Remove from the heat, add the *wakame* and leave to stand for a few minutes before serving.

tip
Dashi miso should not boil or be cooked for a long time, or it will lose its flavour.

Monkfish, chickpea, chorizo & piquillo pepper soup

Serves 4
Preparation: 5 minutes
(including opening jars!)
Cooking time: 15 minutes

Spain produces an enormous range of top-quality jarred and tinned products. Piquillo peppers are one of my favourites. They are a speciality of Navarra in northern Spain. The peppers are smoked over wood charcoal, peeled by hand, marinated and sealed in jars or tins. They taste sweet and strong, with a very addictive light smoky flavour. I am not a fan of tinned chickpeas, which I find taste metallic, but the Spanish jarred chickpeas are excellent. Thanks to the quality of these ingredients, you can produce this amazing soup in 15 minutes!

ingredients
1 chicken stock cube
100 g/3½ oz chorizo, sliced
1 x 570 g/1¼ lb jar of chickpeas
500 g/1 lb 2 oz monkfish (angler fish)
Salt and pepper
3 garlic cloves, crushed
30 g/1¼ oz/1⅓ cup flat-leaf parsley, chopped
100 g/3½ oz piquillo peppers, cut into small strips or squares

method
Place the stock cube, chorizo and 1 litre/1¾ pints of water into a 3-litre soup pan. Bring to a boil and simmer for 5 minutes. Add the chickpeas and simmer for another 5 minutes.

Meanwhile, cut the monkfish into small cubes and season well with salt and freshly ground black pepper. Place the monkfish in the soup. Allow to simmer for 3 minutes. Add the garlic, parsley and peppers and simmer for 2 minutes. Turn off the heat and let it sit for 5 minutes while you set the table. Serve with soft Spanish bread to soak up the juices. Another good recipe for camping.

Middle Eastern black-eyed peas & herb soup

Tahini is a creamy paste made from crushed sesame seeds, an excellent source of calcium and phosphorus. It is the perfect healthy ingredient to have in stock, as it keeps forever. You can use it to flavour soup, make dressings, or hummus of course, but also in desserts. It is what gives this soup its Middle Eastern feel.

ingredients

1 tbsp olive oil
1 large onion, finely chopped
1 large garlic clove, crushed
1 tbsp ground coriander
1 tbsp ground cumin
1 x 400 g/14 oz tin black-eyed peas, drained and rinsed
30 g/1 oz ruby chard
30 g/1 oz watercress
Salt and pepper
1 organic chicken or vegetable stock cube
4 tbsp tahini (sesame seed paste)
75 g/2⅔ oz sun-blush tomatoes
2 tbsp fresh dill, chopped

Lemon and pitta bread, to serve

method

Heat the oil in a 2-litre soup pan, add the onion and fry for 3–4 minutes, until soft and slightly caramelized. Add the garlic and spices and fry for 1 minute. Add the beans, ruby chard and watercress and fry for another minute. Season well with salt and freshly ground black pepper.

Dissolve the stock cube in 1 litre/1¾ pints boiling water. Add to the soup pan, bring to a boil, reduce the heat, and simmer for 5 minutes. Remove from the heat and leave to cool for 10 minutes.

Place half of the soup in a blender. Some oil will settle at the surface of the tahini jar; just stir it well before using. Add half of the tahini, sun-blush tomatoes and dill to the blender. Process until smooth. Repeat with the second batch of ingredients.

Pour the soup back into the saucepan and reheat gently. Serve with lemon and grilled pitta bread.

" You can make this soup with any tinned beans you like. "

Egg & tomato soup

Serves 4
Preparation: 12 minutes
Cooking time: 20 minutes

This is a tomato version of the famous 'Chinese egg-drop' soup. The eggs are literally 'dropped' into the soup from high up. The thin trickle becomes a web of threads in contact with the hot liquid. Even though it tastes delicious, and I have used liquid seasoning to enhance the flavour of the stock cube, my Chinese friends will never forgive me for not using proper stock in this recipe, so if you have a rich homemade stock in your fridge or your freezer, please use it instead! Liquid seasoning is widely available in supermarkets.

ingredients

450 g/1 lb fresh tomatoes
2 tbsp vegetable oil
1 large onion, finely chopped
2 large garlic cloves
20 g/¾ oz fresh ginger, peeled and grated
2 tsp tomato paste
1 chicken or vegetable stock cube
½ tsp liquid seasoning
2 eggs
4 spring onions (scallions), finely chopped
1 small bunch of coriander (cilantro)
Soy sauce or Vietnamese *nuoc nam*, to serve

method

Score the bottom of the tomatoes with a sharp knife. Place the tomatoes in a bowl. Cover with boiling water from the kettle. Leave for 1 minute. You should see the skin slightly detaching from the tomatoes. Drain and rinse in cold water to cool down. Peel the tomatoes, halve them, and remove the seeds with a teaspoon. Chop roughly.

Heat the oil in a 3-litre soup pan. Add the onion and cook for 2 minutes, until soft. Add the garlic and ginger and cook for 1 minute until they start sticking to the bottom of the pan. Add the chopped tomatoes and tomato paste, and cook for about 5 minutes, until they start to soften. Dissolve the stock cube and liquid seasoning in 1 litre/1¾ pints of water and add to the pan (or use a homemade stock if you have some). Bring to a boil, reduce the heat and simmer for 10 minutes.

Break the eggs into a small measuring jug and beat lightly with a fork, until well blended. Hold the jug about 50 cm/20 in above the soup pan. Stir the soup clockwise to create a swirl. Start pouring the eggs slowly while stirring the soup. The egg will form thin strands. Stop stirring when all the egg has been added. Leave to simmer very gently for a minute. Add the spring onions and coriander and remove from the heat.

Leave to sit for 5 minutes and then serve. Each guest can add soy sauce to season the soup to their taste. It is also delicious with Vietnamese *nuoc nam* (see p.25), lime or chilli.

> " *The taste of this soup depends greatly on the quality and ripeness of the tomatoes you use.* "

Cream of rocket & goat's milk

Makes 4 starter or
6 teacup-sized servings
Preparation: 5 minutes
Cooking time: 5 minutes

This is the quickest soup to prepare in this book. There are two advantages to using goat's milk. Many people who have difficulties digesting cow's milk seem to tolerate goat's milk. The second advantage is the wonderful taste.

ingredients

300 g/11 oz rocket leaves (arugula)
750 ml/1¼ pints/generous 3 cups
goat's milk
250 ml/8 fl oz/1 cup double (heavy)
goat's cream
1 tbsp fresh tarragon, chopped
1 tbsp fresh chives, chopped
Salt and pepper
2 tbsp honey, optional

method

Place one-third of the rocket and one-third of the milk in a blender. Whiz until smooth and transfer to a 3-litre saucepan. Repeat with the rest of the rocket and goat's milk. Add the goat's cream, tarragon and chives to the saucepan. Bring gently to just below simmering. Season to taste with salt and plenty of freshly ground black pepper.

The soup will slightly thicken when heated, giving it a beautiful consistency of double cream.

If desired, pour the soup into teacups, drizzle with about ½ tsp honey, stir and serve.

❛❛ Just 10 minutes for a soup good enough to grace a top restaurant menu. ❜❜

Couscous, harissa & herbs

Serves 4
Preparation: 5 minutes
Cooking time: 15 minutes

Watch out! This soup is extremely spicy and definitely for chilli addicts. Try to get a good-quality harissa from a Moroccan grocery store or in the speciality corner of your supermarket. I have included a really nice recipe for harissa, which you can keep in the fridge for 1 month (see p.185). There are many different qualities of couscous and, again, try to get hold of a North African brand with a medium-grain.

ingredients
2 tbsp olive oil
4 garlic cloves, crushed
1–2 tbsp harissa
75 g/2²⁄₃ oz medium-grain couscous
1 chicken stock cube
15 g/½ oz/¼ cup fresh mint, chopped
15 g/½ oz/¼ cup fresh coriander (cilantro), chopped

tip
Great with leftover fish or chicken.

method
Heat the oil in a 3-litre soup pan. Fry the garlic over medium heat for less than a minute. It should be golden but not brown. Add the harissa and couscous and fry for 30 seconds. Dissolve the stock cubes in 1.2 litres/2 pints boiling water from the kettle and add to the soup. Bring to a boil, reduce the heat, and simmer for 7–8 minutes.

Turn off the heat. Add the mint and coriander and leave to infuse for 3–4 minutes. Serve.

" Replace some of the harissa with tomato paste if your tastebuds cannot handle hot, hot, HOT! "

Cream of butterbean with tapenade dressing

Serves 4
Preparation: 5 minutes
Cooking time: 15 minutes
+ 10 minutes cooling time

Beans give a beautiful creamy texture to soups. Make sure you always thoroughly rinse tinned beans, to remove the excess sodium as well as the unpleasant taste from the tin that might ruin your soup. The best way to do it is to drain the beans in a colander and wash them under running water. Tapenade is an olive and anchovy paste you can buy ready-made from most supermarkets. Vegetarians can substitute capers for the tapenade.

ingredients
1 tbsp olive oil
2 large garlic cloves
1 sprig rosemary
3 x 420 g/15 oz tins butterbeans (lima beans), drained and rinsed well
1 vegetable stock cube

for the tapenade dressing
2 tbsp chives, finely chopped
2 tbsp tapenade (or capers, for the vegetarian option)
1 tsp balsamic vinegar
2 tbsp extra-virgin olive oil

method
Heat the oil in a heavy 3-litre soup pan. Fry the garlic and rosemary over medium heat for 1 minute. The garlic should be slightly golden but not burnt, or it will give a bitter taste to the soup. Add the butterbeans, 900 ml/1½ pints of water and the stock cube. Bring to a boil, reduce the heat, and simmer for 10 minutes.

Meanwhile, finely chop the chives and mix with the tapenade, balsamic vinegar and olive oil. Set aside.

Leave the butterbean soup to cool down for 10–15 minutes. Place half of it in a blender and whiz until smooth. Pour the contents into a sieve placed over a saucepan. Repeat with the other half of the soup. Stir and press the soup through the sieve to extract as much liquid as possible and remove the rough skins of the beans.

Reheat gently and serve topped with a tablespoon of the dressing.

Thai rainbow trout & coconut soup

Serves 4
Preparation: 5 minutes
Cooking time: 15 minutes

I use a store-bought curry paste for this soup to speed up the preparation. Each brand is different and the amount given in the recipe is a rough indication. Everyone reacts differently to chilli, and you might want to adapt the quantity to your taste. I have included a recipe for a homemade red curry paste (p.182). It is easy to make if you have a food processor and you can keep it in the fridge for up to 2 weeks.

ingredients
2 x 400 ml/14 fl oz tins reduced-fat coconut milk
1 chicken stock cube
1 tbsp Demerara (turbinado) sugar
About 2 tbsp Thai red curry paste (for homemade, see p.182)
120 g/4 oz Chinese (Napa) cabbage leaves, finely shredded
500 g/1 lb 2 oz rainbow trout, skinned and cut into 4 cm/1½ in pieces
1 tsp fresh green peppercorns, crushed, or ½ tsp freshly ground black pepper

Thai basil or coriander (cilantro), to garnish
Fish sauce and lime juice, to season

method
Place the coconut milk, stock cube and sugar in a 3-litre soup pan. Fill one of the tins with water and add this to the pan. Bring to a simmer, stirring constantly so that the coconut doesn't curdle.

Dilute the curry paste in a ladle of soup, then add it gradually. Taste and check if you need to add any more, bearing in mind that you will be adding fresh pepper. Add the cabbage leaves and boil for 3 minutes. Add the trout pieces and the crushed fresh peppercorn or freshly ground black pepper and boil for another 3 minutes.

Place the Thai basil leaves or coriander at the bottom of the serving plates. Divide the soup between the plates, season with fish sauce and lime juice, and serve.

66 Perfect for a stylish improvised dinner with friends. 99

Smoked haddock soup with sourdough croutons

Serves 4 generously
Preparation: 5 minutes
Cooking time: 17 minutes

Smoked haddock keeps well, cooks quickly, and is perfect for an improvised soup. I prefer the un-dyed smoked haddock that hasn't been artificially coloured or flavoured. It has a light amber colour and is more subtle in taste. It should be slightly rigid and glossy, with no extensive gap in the flesh or discoloration.

ingredients

650 g/1 lb 7 oz smoked haddock
1 x 400 ml/14 fl oz tin evaporated milk
1 small leek, finely sliced
3 garlic cloves, crushed
1 bay leaf
200 g/7 oz sourdough bread
Olive oil, for drizzling
30 g/1 oz parsley, roughly chopped
Freshly ground black pepper

method

Preheat the oven to 220°C/425°F/Gas Mark 7.

Cut the haddock into two chunks. Place them in a heavy 3-litre pan. Cover with evaporated milk and, using the tin as a measuring jug, add 3 tins of water. Add the sliced leek, crushed garlic and bay leaf. Bring to a simmer (not to a boil), and keep the mixture simmering for 10–12 minutes.

Meanwhile, cut the bread into 1½ cm/¾ in slices, then cut each slice into 4, to make big croutons. Place on a baking tray, drizzle with olive oil and bake for 10 minutes, flipping them halfway through. They should be golden and well toasted.

Back to the soup. At this point, lift the pieces of haddock with a slotted spoon and place on a large plate. Detach the skin, being careful not to flake the fish too much, as it is nice to keep large chunks. Return them to the soup. Add the chopped parsley and freshly ground pepper and simmer for 2 more minutes. Adjust the seasoning. Divide the toasted bread chunks between the plates, ladle the soup and fish over the bread, and serve.

heaven
for pennies

What I like about budget cooking is that it makes you more resourceful. You won't throw away vegetable peels once you've discovered they make delicious stocks. If you live near the coast, you can pick up clams at low tide for nothing. Open your fridge and you will discover that the wilted lettuce you wouldn't use in a salad will taste wonderful in a soup. The Parmesan crust that you have grated to the bone can be thrown in for extra flavour. A spoonful of that wholegrain mustard will transform your parsnip soup.

Don't underestimate your spice rack. The spices that you bought a few months ago to make that special curry can really transform a soup. If you don't have any spices, get them in packets from an Indian or Middle Eastern shop. They will be cheaper and go a long way.

You can also balance your costs to keep within budget. Some of the soups will seem more expensive than others. Arborio rice and pecans are expensive ingredients, but if you combine them with leeks and milk, you will have a delicious, cheap soup. Another good way to keep the cost down is to browse through the recipes and match ingredients you already have and don't need to buy.

You will find in this chapter a variety of soups to suit different budgets, though not all the costs will be as low as the cream of onion soup, which will feed four people for next to nothing!

Salt cod, tomato & paprika soup

Serves 4
Preparation: 24 hours to
soak the cod + 10 minutes
Cooking time: about 1 hour

Salt cod is cheaper if purchased in Portuguese and Spanish specialty shops. It is easier to handle if cut into small pieces – ask the shopkeeper to do it for you, as it's a tough job. It should be thick and white, not yellowish. It will keep for a few months and is a handy ingredient to stock in your fridge in an airtight container. Salt cod is no longer salty after it has been soaked for 24 hours, but meaty and firm, and it will give a unique flavour to your soup.

ingredients

450 g/1 lb salt cod pieces, with bones
500 g/1 lb 2 oz fresh tomatoes, peeled and quartered
1 x 400 g/14 oz tin peeled tomatoes, preferably Italian, halved
6 garlic cloves
Salt and pepper
1 tsp sugar
2 tbsp olive oil
1 tsp paprika
8 slices of ciabatta bread (2 slices per person)
15 g/½ oz/¼ cup flat-leaf parsley, chopped

Extra-virgin olive oil, for drizzling

method

Rinse the cod well under running water. Place in a large non-metallic bowl and cover with plenty of cold water. Soak for 24 hours, changing the water about 5 times.

Preheat the oven to 200ºC/ 400ºF/Gas Mark 6.

Place the fresh and tinned tomatoes in an oven dish, add the garlic cloves and season with salt and freshly ground black pepper. Sprinkle with sugar, drizzle with 1 tablespoon of olive oil, and bake for 45 minutes.

Take the tomatoes from the oven. Remove the garlic cloves and place on a chopping board. Press with a spoon to extract the pulp. Discard the peel.

Remove the cod pieces from the water and drain on kitchen paper.

Heat the remaining oil in a 3-litre soup pan. Add the garlic pulp and fry gently for 2–3 minutes. Add the baked tomatoes and the paprika, and stir. Add 800 ml/ 1½ pints of water and bring to a simmer. Add the cod pieces and cook gently for 15 minutes.

Meanwhile, preheat the grill and toast the ciabatta slices for 10 minutes, until well browned on both sides.

Lift the cod pieces from the soup with a slotted spoon. Using 2 forks, remove the skin and bones and break into chunks. Place back into the soup and continue to simmer for 5 minutes. Check the seasoning, but it should be salty enough.

To serve, place two pieces of ciabatta at the bottom of each soup plate, sprinkle with chopped parsley, and pour the soup over. Drizzle with extra-virgin olive oil.

Lentil soup with caramelized onions

Serves 4
Preparation: 20 minutes
Cooking time: 1 hour and 10 minutes

Unlike beans, lentils do not need soaking, which makes them easier to use. There are many varieties, each with their own taste and cooking time. I have made this soup with green lentils, but any lentils can be used. Just refer to the packet for the cooking time and add a few minutes because in a soup they should be a bit more mushy.

for the soup
1 onion
1 leek, washed well
1 large carrot
1 celery stick
2 tbsp olive oil
1 garlic clove, crushed
175 g/6 oz/scant 2 cups green lentils

for the caramelized onions
4 medium onions
2 tbsp olive oil
½ tsp sugar
Salt and pepper

Horseradish cream, to serve

tip
Straining a stock can be more tricky than it appears. Liquids can run along the side of the pot, miss the strainer and go straight into the sink. Solids can suddenly tumble out, splashing the burning hot stock. To avoid all this misery, just ladle the stock through a strainer placed over your soup pan.

method
Peel and trim the onion, leek, carrot and celery. Place the peels and trimmings in a 2-litre saucepan and cover with 1.3 litres/2¼ pints of water. Bring to a boil, reduce the heat and simmer, partly covered, for 30 minutes.

Meanwhile, finely chop the vegetables and set aside.

Start making the caramelized onions. Finely chop the onions. Heat the oil in a large frying pan and cook the onions over a medium heat for 2 minutes, until soft. Sprinkle with sugar, stir well, and cover. If you don't have a lid that fits, just cover with a large piece of foil. Simmer, covered, for 30–40 minutes, stirring and checking regularly that nothing burns.

Meanwhile, heat 2 tablespoons of oil in a 3-litre soup pan. Add the chopped vegetables and cook over a medium heat for 10 minutes, until soft and slightly caramelized. Add the crushed garlic and lentils and stir until well coated with oil. Do not season with salt: it will toughen the lentil skins and they will take longer to cook. By now, the stock will be ready. Place a strainer over the soup pan and ladle the stock directly into it. Bring to a boil, boil vigorously for 2–3 minutes, and skim off the grey foam that rises to the surface. Reduce the heat and simmer for 25–30 minutes, until the lentils are tender.

Keep an eye on the onions and season them. They should be starting to brown. Check that the heat is very low (use a heat diffuser if needed). Let them cook slowly until the soup is ready. They should be golden brown with crisp edges.

When the soup is ready, you can leave it as it is, or leave it to cool for 10 minutes and partly blend with an electric hand-held blender. Serve the soup topped with the caramelized onions and some horseradish cream.

Roasted garlic & bread soup

Serves 4
Preparation: 5 minutes
Cooking time: 45 minutes

This is obviously for garlic lovers. It is also a 'poor man's soup' when all you have in the house is garlic, bread and eggs! In the southwest of France, it was traditionally served to newlyweds on their wedding night. Jokers would erupt into their room in the middle of the night and force the newlyweds to eat the soup out of a pot – yes, that one. If you survived that wedding night, you could survive anything.

ingredients
4 heads of garlic
Salt
3 tbsp duck fat, or olive oil
150 g/5 oz mixture of any bread (sourdough, wholewheat, corn bread), cut into small chunks
4 eggs
30 g/1 oz/½ cup flat-leaf parsley, chopped

method
Preheat the oven to 190°C/375°F/Gas Mark 5.

Wash the garlic and cut each head in half horizontally. Place them on a baking tray, sprinkle with salt, and drizzle with the duck fat or olive oil. Bake for 20 minutes; they should be golden brown. Remove from the oven and place them, as they are, in a 3 litre saucepan. Add 1.4 litres/2½ pints of water, cover and simmer over a low heat for 20 minutes.

Meanwhile, toast the bread pieces under a grill for 10–15 minutes, turning them halfway through. They should be well browned and dry. Set aside.

When the garlic soup is ready, press on the garlic heads with a potato masher so that the cloves are released into the stock and partly mashed. Ladle the stock and garlic into a sieve set over a 3-litre soup pan. Press well on the garlic heads to extract maximum juices and garlic pulp.

Return the garlic stock to a boil. Add the bread and bring to a simmer. Break each egg, one at a time, into a tea cup and gently pour each one into the soup. Simmer for 5 minutes if you like soft eggs; 2 more minutes if you like them firmer.

Place some chopped parsley at the bottom of each soup plate. Lift the eggs with a large spoon and place in the soup plates, being careful not to break them. Pour some of the soup over each and serve at once.

" Choose plump garlic heads with firm cloves and purple toned skin. "

Fish soup with toasted vermicelli & aïoli

Serves 4
Preparation: 15 minutes
Cooking time: 1 hour

Ask your fishmonger for fish bones and, if he knows you well enough, they will be free. Just don't use the bones from oily fish. This soup is almost a meal in itself. Don't worry if you've never made aïoli before, the recipe at the end of the book is foolproof (see p.184).

tip

Toasting the vermicelli before adding it to soups gives it a lovely nutty flavour.

method

Use a large, 5-litre soup pan because you will need to fit in a large volume of fish heads. Cut the fish parts into small pieces with good kitchen scissors.

Heat the oil. Add the onion, fennel, carrot and garlic, and cook over a medium heat for 4−5 minutes. The vegetables should start to caramelize, but do not let them brown. Season well and add the tomato paste. Cook for another minute. Add the white wine, and stir well to scrape off the caramelized bits. Leave to cook and reduce for about 2 minutes.

Add one-third of the fish trimmings, and cook over high heat until well blended with the vegetables. Then add another third, cook it well, and finally the last of the fish. Season well. Add 2 litres/3½ pints of water and bring to a boil. Skim the foam that rises to the surface and simmer, partly covered, for 20 minutes.

Meanwhile, crush the vermicelli between your fingers into small pieces. Place in a heated frying pan. Dry-fry over a medium heat for 3−4 minutes, until slightly golden and fragrant. Place in a bowl and leave to cool.

Back to the soup. Using a potato masher, press on the fish to break down all the pieces and really mix them up. Add the mussels and cook for 4 minutes. Turn off the heat and leave the soup to cool for 10 minutes.

Remove the mussels from the soup, discard the shells, then return to the soup. Place a sieve on top of a pan. Ladle some of the stock into the sieve. Stir and press well, to extract as much juice as possible. Repeat with the rest of the soup.

Return the stock to a simmer, and cook for 10−12 minutes to reduce it and concentrate the flavours. Adjust the seasoning, add the toasted vermicelli, and simmer for 5 minutes, just long enough to cook the vermicelli.

Toast the slices of bread, generously spread with aïoli, and serve with the soup.

ingredients

1.5 kg/3 lb 6 oz fish trimmings
(heads, bones, tails)
2 tbsp olive oil
1 red onion, sliced
130 g/4½ oz fennel,
finely sliced
130 g/4½ oz carrot,
finely chopped
4 garlic cloves, peeled and
roughly chopped
Salt and pepper
2 tbsp tomato paste
100 ml/3½ fl oz/
scant ½ cup white wine
130 g/4½ oz vermicelli
200 g/7 oz mussels

Aïoli (p.184) and toasted
bread, to serve

Clam chowder

Serves 4
Preparation: At least 3 hours
to soak + 10 minutes
Cooking time: 25 minutes

Clam chowder evokes the seaside and early morning clam-picking. This is exactly what we did when we prepared this soup for photography. If you pick your own clams, you need to scrub them first, then soak them for at least 3 hours. If you leave them in water, they will slowly purge themselves of all the sand and grit they contain. It is fine to leave them all day in the water if needed. The same applies if you buy clams from the fishmonger: they will need soaking. Some people soak clams in salted water. I find that clear water, changed regularly, works just as well, and you don't waste salt.

for the clams
1.5 kg/3 lb 6 oz clams
15g/½ oz/1 tbsp butter
1 tbsp olive oil
50 g/2 oz/⅓ cup shallots, chopped
1 celery stick, sliced

for the soup
2 tbsp olive oil
75 g/3 oz/¼ cup bacon, chopped
1 large onion, peeled and cubed
400 g/14 oz potatoes, peeled and cubed
1 x 400 ml/14 fl oz tin evaporated milk
1 tbsp cornflour (cornstarch)

tip
Discard any broken or opened clams prior to cooking and any that have remained closed after cooking. None of these are safe to eat. The same is true for mussels.

method
Scrub the clams and let them soak in water for at least 3 hours. Then drain and clean again under cold running water. Discard any broken or open ones.

Heat the butter and oil in a 4-litre pot fitted with a lid. Add the shallots and celery, and cook over a medium heat for 2 minutes, until soft. Add the clams, cover, and cook over high heat for 3 minutes, shaking the pan from time to time. Turn off the heat and leave the clams to cook in their steam for a minute longer.

Ladle the clams into a strainer set over a bowl to collect the cooking juices. Leave the clams to cool in the strainer. Pass the cooking juice through a very fine sieve to get rid of any remaining sand.

For the soup, heat the oil in a heavy 3-litre soup pot, and fry the bacon until slightly crispy. Remove the bacon and set aside. In the bacon fat, fry the onion for 3–4 minutes, until soft and slightly coloured. Add the potatoes, and fry for 1 more minute. Add 500 ml/18 fl oz/generous 2 cups of water and cook for 15 minutes, until the potatoes are soft. Add the evaporated milk, clam cooking juices, and bacon, then bring to a simmer.

Shell the clams, and as you shell them, drop them directly into the soup. Discard any closed ones. Simmer for 1 minute.

Dilute the cornflour in a tablespoon of water and add to the soup, stirring constantly. This will thicken the soup and give it the consistency of double cream. Simmer gently for 2–3 minutes. The soup is ready to serve.

Congee

Serves 4–6
Preparation: 5 minutes
Cooking time: 2½ hours

Congee is the Chinese equivalent of porridge. I had a bowl of congee every morning in Beijing and it gave me energy for most of the day. Rice is cooked for hours until it turns into a thick white soup. Congee is very nourishing and very easy to digest. It is also the perfect evening soup when you are not feeling well or to soothe a stomachache.

ingredients

200 g/7 oz ham bone
160 g/5½ oz raw spare ribs
30 g/1 oz piece ginger, peeled
2 large spring onions (scallions)
1 piece of Chinese dried mandarin peel,
or 5 cm/2 in fresh mandarin peel
140 g/4½ oz/¾ cup Thai jasmine rice
(or a mixture of 100 g/3½ oz/
½ cup jasmine rice and 40 g/
1½ oz/scant ½ cup glutinous rice

Pickled cabbage, chopped streaky
(lean) bacon, and fresh coriander
(cilantro), to garnish

method

Place all the ingredients in a 3-litre soup pan, cover with 2 litres/3½ pints of cold water, and slowly bring to a boil, stirring occasionally so that the rice does not stick to the bottom.

Once it has reached boiling stage, reduce the heat, and simmer, partly covered, over very low heat for 2½ hours, stirring occasionally.

Remove the bones, ginger and mandarin peel. Serve garnished with the pickled cabbages, pan-fried chopped streaky bacon, and coriander.

Spuds, onion, bacon & cheese soup

Serves 4
Preparation: 10 minutes
Cooking time: 25 minutes

I have a soft spot for Irish potatoes. Their texture is so fluffy and creamy that they are perfect for soups. If you can get hold of Irish potatoes, use baking potatoes. This soup is filling enough to serve as a main course.

ingredients
500 g/1 lb 2 oz Irish potatoes, finely chopped
600 ml/1 pint/2½ cups milk
2 tbsp olive oil
2 onions, finely sliced
Salt and pepper
125 g/4 oz smoked back (Canadian) bacon, thinly sliced
100 g/3½ oz/1 cup mature (sharp) Cheddar cheese, grated

A whole nutmeg and black pepper, to serve

method
Place the potatoes in a 3-litre soup pan. Add the milk and 600 ml/1 pint of water. Bring to a boil, then simmer for 15 minutes.

Meanwhile, heat the oil in a medium-sized frying pan. Add the onions, and fry over medium to low heat for 10 minutes. They should be soft and really golden brown. Season well, add to the soup and cook for 10 more minutes. In the same frying pan, cook the bacon for a couple of minutes, until crisp on the edges. Add this to the soup too.

Turn off the heat under the soup. Add the cheese and let the soup sit while the cheese melts slightly. Set the table with the nutmeg and a grater and serve up, with plenty of freshly ground black pepper.

Cook this soup whenever it is miserable outside, and you will feel wonderful.

Turkish chicken & yoghurt soup with golden butter

Serves 4
Preparation: 2 hours
to make the stock
Cooking time: 12 minutes

Golden butter is butter that is cooked over a very low heat until it turns golden and acquires a 'hazelnut' aftertaste. That is why the French call it '*beurre noisette*'. It is a crucial ingredient in Turkish cooking. It is almost like a spice. Here it is used like olive oil to drizzle on top of the soup at the last moment. The quality of the chicken stock is crucial. Mint is added at the end for a kick. You can add fresh mint, but I find dried mint makes the soup taste more authentic.

ingredients

1.5 kg/3 lb 6 oz chicken wings
1 large onion, peeled and cut into wedges
1 large carrot, peeled and cut into chunks
1 medium-sized red chilli, halved
Salt
85 g/3 oz/¾ stick unsalted butter
40 g/1½ oz/scant ½ cup basmati rice
2 tbsp cornflour (cornstarch)
500 g/1 lb 2 oz yoghurt
1 large egg + 1 egg yolk
1 tsp dried mint
Paprika, to garnish

tip

To reheat this soup, stir it all the time and do not let it boil or it will curdle.

method

Preheat the oven to 220°C/425°F/Gas Mark 7.

To make the stock, place the chicken wings on a roasting dish, add the onion, carrot and chilli, and roast for 45 minutes. Five minutes before the end of the cooking time, season well with salt.

Remove some of the meat from the chicken wings and set aside. Place the rest in a 3-litre pan. Deglaze the dish with 250 ml/9 fl oz/generous 1 cup of boiling water from the kettle, scraping the bottom to detach any bits, and pour into the pan. Add 1.6 litres/2¾ pints of water, bring to a boil and simmer gently for 1 hour. This stock needs to be more concentrated than usual. It is cooked uncovered and reduced by almost half. At the end of the hour, you should obtain 1 litre.

Meanwhile, make the golden butter. Place the butter into a small pan over a very low heat. Let it cook for about 10 minutes, until it becomes golden. The timing is a bit tricky. Once the butter starts to take on that golden tone, it can quickly burn. Watch it carefully. Your nose will be the best judge. If you spot a change in smell from sweet to acrid, immediately transfer the butter to a bowl and set aside.

When the soup is ready, strain the stock, skim the fat off the surface and bring back to a boil. Add the rice and simmer, covered, for 10 minutes. Mix the cornflour with 2 tbsp water. Add to the stock and stir well for a minute, until slightly thickened. Whisk the yoghurt, egg and egg yolk until well blended. Slowly pour the mixture into the simmering soup, whisking all the time to avoid curdling. Add the dried mint and the reserved chicken meat, and let it simmer very gently for 5 minutes, stirring all the time.

Pour the soup into bowls, drizzle some hazelnut butter on top, and sprinkle with paprika. Serve with grilled pitta bread.

Minty & spicy broad bean soup

Serves 4
Preparation: 10 minutes
Cooking time: 20 minutes

Broad beans are lovely when they have been freshly picked. I have been very disappointed these past few years with the quality of broad beans available in shops. They are often floury and bitter. This is why I would recommend buying frozen young broad beans for this soup unless, of course, you grow your own.

ingredients
30 g/1 oz fresh mint
2 tbsp olive oil
1 large onion, peeled and finely chopped
1 carrot, peeled and finely chopped
2 tsp mustard seeds
1 tsp cumin seeds
6 cardamons, crushed
¼ tsp turmeric
Large pinch of chilli powder
500 g/1 lb 2 oz frozen young broad (fava) beans

method
Bring 1.3 litres/2¼ pints of water to a boil. Add the mint, turn off the heat and leave to infuse for 10 minutes.

Meanwhile, heat the oil in a 3-litre soup pan and fry the onion and carrot for 5 minutes over a medium heat, until soft. Add the spices and fry for 1 more minute, over a low heat, until they are well coated and caramelized.

Add the broad beans and stir well. Add the mint-infused water, bring to a boil and simmer for 15 minutes. Turn off the heat and leave to cool slightly.

Whizz the broad beans and stock in the blender in 3 batches. Pass through a fine sieve to remove all the skin. Reheat and serve.

" A simple mint infused water gives this soup its fresh, summery taste. "

Roast parsnip soup with grain mustard & nutmeg cream

Serves 4
Preparation: 10 minutes
Cooking time: 35 minutes

Strangely, parsnips had disappeared from the markets when I was growing up in France. Now they are back as a trendy item with the label 'forgotten vegetable'. They were a real taste discovery when I moved to England. Like carrots, parsnips are truly delicious when they are roasted. This is why I have used a similar cooking technique to the roasted carrot soup (p.65).

ingredients

1 kg/2¼ lb parsnips
1 onion
2 tbsp olive oil
Salt and pepper

to serve

125 ml/4 fl oz/½ cup single (light) cream
1 tbsp grain mustard
¼ tsp freshly grated nutmeg

method

Preheat the oven to 200°C/400°F/Gas Mark 6.

Wash the parsnips, peel them, quarter them and core them. Place the peels and cores in a 3-litre soup pan. Discard the outer brown peel from the onion, which would give your stock a bitter taste, but add to the pan the tender outer layer that you remove before chopping the onion. Cover the parsnips and onion peels with 1.5 litres/2⅔ pints of water, bring to a boil, and simmer for 30 minutes.

Slice your onion into wedges. Place the onion wedges and parsnips on a baking tray, drizzle with 2 tablespoons of olive oil and bake for 30 minutes. Stir and season halfway through. Remove from the oven and leave to cool slightly. Turn off the heat under the parsnip stock and leave to cool.

Place one-third of the parsnips in the blender, add about 400 ml/14 fl oz/ 1¾ cups of parsnip stock and whizz until well blended. Proceed in the same way with the rest. Place in a saucepan and season. Add more stock if you want a thinner soup. Reheat gently.

Mix the cream, mustard and nutmeg until well blended. Serve the soup in bowls with a large spoonful of mustard cream on top.

Dairy-free cream of onion with Worcestershire sauce

Serves 4
Preparation: 15 minutes
Cooking time: 1 hour

I wanted to create an onion soup that would have a strong British identity and do justice to the delicious onions grown in England. This soup is beautifully creamy with the kick from the Worcestershire sauce just coming through. Oat cream brings in creaminess without heaviness and really complements the onion taste.

ingredients

1 kg/2¼ lb onions
50 g/2 oz/½ stick butter
3 tbsp olive oil
2 tomatoes
1 tsp sugar
3 garlic cloves, crushed
Salt and pepper
1½ tbsp Worcestershire sauce
250 ml/9 fl oz/1 cup oat cream

Toasted bread and Marmite, to serve

tip

Onion soup oxidizes quickly and does not keep well. Store in the fridge for no more than two days, or freeze as soon as possible.

method

Peel, halve and finely slice the onions. Heat the butter and oil in a 3-litre soup pan. Add the onions and fry over a medium heat for 2–3 minutes, until soft, stirring and checking occasionally that the edges and bottom do not burn.

Place the tomatoes in a small bowl and cover with boiling water for 1 minute. Drain, then rinse under cold water so they cool down and you don't burn yourself. Peel, core and seed the tomatoes. Chop roughly and add to the onions, along with the sugar and the garlic.

Cover the pan and cook gently for 30 minutes, checking regularly that nothing burns. The onions should cook slowly and become golden gradually without reaching a dark caramel colour. Adjust the heat and cook 10 minutes more if needed. Season with salt, pepper, and 1½ tbsp of Worcestershire sauce, and cook, still covered, for 10 more minutes. Add 800 ml/1¼ pints of water and simmer, half covered, for 20 minutes.

Turn off the heat and set aside for 10 minutes to cool slightly. Partly whiz the soup with an electric hand-held mixer. You should leave some onion bits. Add the oat cream and stir well. Check the seasoning and add more Worcestershire sauce if needed.

Serve with Marmite toast.

Lettuce soup with pancetta

Serves 4
Preparation: 15 minutes
Cooking time: 40 minutes

If you have leftover wilted lettuces in your fridge, do not throw them in the bin, throw them in this soup. Round lettuce, batavia, oak leaf, radicchio, rocket – anything goes: the greater the variety, the more interesting the soup will be.

ingredients
2 tbsp olive oil
150 g/5 oz Italian smoked pancetta, cut into small lardons
1 onion, finely sliced
150 g/5 oz celery, finely chopped
250 g/9 oz baking potatoes
Freshly ground black pepper
35 g/1¼ oz Parmesan crust
250 g /9 oz wilted lettuces, roughly chopped
150 g/5 oz leftover or cooked sausages, chopped

method
Heat 1 tablespoon of the olive oil in a 3-litre pan. Add the pancetta, and cook for 2 minutes until slightly crispy. Add the vegetables, and cook for 6–7 minutes, until soft. Season well with pepper, not salt, as the pancetta and Parmesan should be enough to salt the stock. Cover with 1.3 litres/2¼ pints of water, bring to a boil, add the Parmesan crust and simmer, partly covered, for 30 minutes.

In a large frying pan, heat the rest of the oil, add the wilted lettuces, and pan-fry for 2 minutes. Season lightly. Add the lettuces and cooked sausages to the soup and cook for 5 minutes.

Turn off the heat. Remove the Parmesan crust.

tip
Keep your Parmesan cheese crusts to add extra flavour to soups. Cover them with olive oil and in a few days you will have a delicious Parmesan oil.

Good old-fashioned vegetable soup with watercress butter

Serves 4
Preparation: 15 minutes
Cooking time: 50 minutes

There is nothing more comforting than a classic grandma-style vegetable soup. As usual, I like to make a stock out of the vegetable peels and trimmings for extra flavour, but it is also delicious made with water if you are short on time. Watercress butter is ultra-simple to prepare and makes a stunning garnish for vegetable soups.

for the soup
2 tbsp olive oil
1 large onion
125 g/4 oz carrot
125 g/4 oz leek
1 celery stick
150 g/5 oz swede
200 g/7 oz baking potato
Salt and pepper

for the watercress butter
30 g/1 oz watercress leaves
(large stalks removed)
65 g/2½ oz/generous ½ stick butter,
at room temperature
Salt and pepper

method

Wash all the vegetables well. Peel and trim. Place the peels and trimmings in a 3-litre pot, add 1.3 litres/2¼ pints of water and cook, partly covered, for 30 minutes.

Meanwhile, finely chop the peeled vegetables and set aside.

Prepare the watercress butter. Finely chop the watercress, add to the butter and mix well with a fork. Season with salt and freshly ground black pepper. Keep refrigerated.

Heat the oil in a 3-litre pan. Add the vegetables and cook for 10–12 minutes, until softened. Season well with salt and pepper. Add the trimming stock and bring to a boil. Reduce the heat and simmer, partly covered, for 30 minutes.

You can serve the soup as it is, with chunky vegetables, or partly blend it with an electric hand-held mixer. Serve it topped with a tablespoon of watercress butter that will slowly melt into the soup.

Creamy leek & pecan soup

Serves 4–6
Preparation: 10 minutes
Cooking time: 33 minutes

Pecan nuts are not used as much as they should be in savoury dishes. They give a very autumnal feel to this leek soup. Pecans quickly become rancid, so the best way to store them is in an airtight container: 3 months in your cupboard, 6 months in the fridge, or up to 2 years in the freezer.

ingredients

2 tbsp olive oil
500 g/1 lb 2 oz leeks, finely chopped
Salt and pepper
35 g/1¼ oz/ generous ⅛ cup Arborio (risotto) rice
85 g/3 oz/½ cup pecans
600 ml/1 pint/2½ cups milk

method

Heat the oil in a 3-litre stock pan. Fry the leeks over a medium heat for 2 minutes, then reduce the heat and cook for 10 minutes, stirring occasionally. They should start to caramelize. Season halfway through cooking.

Add the Arborio rice and pecans, then the milk and 750 ml/1¼ pints of water. Bring to a simmer, not a boil, and simmer very slowly (use a heat diffuser if needed) for 30 minutes. Don't worry if the heat has curdled the milk, it will become smooth again when blended.

You can serve this soup blended or half-blended. In either case, leave the soup to cool slightly to avoid burning yourself with splashes. To blend into a creamy soup, place in the blender and process in three batches. To retain some consistency, partly blend the soup using an electric hand-held blender. It is very nice to munch on pecans that have been softened and almost sweetened in the cooking liquid.

tip

Like onion soup, leek soup doesn't keep well — it's best to freeze any leftovers.

66 *This soup is very rich and should be served in smaller quantities.* 99

power lunch

A warm cup of soup is much more satisfying and nutritious than a sandwich. Thanks to Thermos flasks, you can carry soups anywhere, not just to the office. They are perfect in the car, on the train, when hiking, or even when out fishing.

These soups are designed for optimum nutrition. They will keep you going for the rest of the day. Soups are an easy way to vary a healthy diet. You can use sprouted seeds as a garnish, brown rice to replace pasta in a minestrone, chestnuts and oats to give body to your mushroom soup. I have also shared my secret remedy against any developing lurgies: chicken, tomato, garlic and ginger soup.

The second half of the chapter is dedicated to soups for one. These are quick to make. Some of them can even be cooked in the morning before you go out or quickly put together just before lunch. They are also useful if you are single and don't want to eat the same soup four days in a row. The emphasis is again on nutrition, using five-star ingredients like broccoli, red lentils, red pepper and quinoa. These soups are vegetarian but can easily be complemented with leftover chicken, fish or smoked fish.

Minestrone with brown rice, sage & lemon zest

Serves 4
Preparation: 20 minutes
Cooking time: about 1 hour

Brown rice and the fresh flavours of sage and lemon zest put a spin on this minestrone that will energize you for the rest of the day. You can freeze it in individual containers. You might add some chorizo to one, or some flash-fried prawns (shrimp) to another, to vary your lunches.

ingredients

1 onion
1 small carrot
1 small leek
1 large celery stalk
1 small courgette (zucchini)
35 g/1½ oz *cavolo nero* or kale
100 g/3½ oz broccoli
8–10 sage leaves
Grated zest of ½ lemon
3 tbsp grated Parmesan
2 tbsp olive oil
40 g/1½ oz/scant ½ cup brown rice
1 ripe tomato, chopped
½ x 400 g/14 oz tin borlotti (cranberry) beans, drained and rinsed

Extra-virgin olive oil, to serve

method

Wash all the vegetables well. Peel and trim the onion (discard the outer brown skin that would give a bitter taste to the stock). Peel and trim the carrots and leek. Trim the celery and courgette. Reserve the peels and trimmings to make your vegetable stock: place them in a 3-litre saucepan, cover with 1.5 litres/2¾ pints of water, and simmer for 30 minutes.

Meanwhile, finely chop the peeled vegetables, courgette, *cavolo nero* and broccoli. Finely chop the sage leaves and mix them with the lemon zest and Parmesan.

Heat 1 tablespoon of olive oil in a second 3-litre saucepan, and add the chopped onion, carrot, leek and celery. Let them cook slowly for 15 minutes. Season halfway through. By now, your stock will be ready.

Add the rice and chopped tomato to the vegetables, strain the stock directly on top of the vegetables and simmer, partly covered, for 25 minutes.

Rinse the stock pan and heat 1 tablespoon of olive oil in it. Add the *cavolo nero* or kale, courgette and broccoli and stir-fry for 2 minutes. Add to the soup along with the borlotti beans and the sage mixture. Simmer for another 2 minutes. The green vegetables should still be a little crunchy. The soup is ready. Serve with a dash of extra-virgin olive oil.

Roasted carrots with sprouted seed pesto

Serves 4
Preparation: 20 minutes
Cooking time: 45 minutes –
1 hour

While writing this book, I tried out different ways of cooking carrots, and I have a strong preference for the taste of carrots that have been roasted. To add even more carrot flavour, I make a carrot stock out of the trimmings. Assorted sprouted seeds are easy to find in health-food shops and some supermarkets. You could also get a sprouter and make your own.

for the soup
850 g/1¾ lb carrots
1 onion
4 garlic cloves
2 x 5 cm/2 in orange peels
1 tsp coriander seeds
1 tbsp olive oil
Salt and pepper

for the sprouted seed pesto
50 g/2 oz sprouted seeds
85 g/3 oz pimiento-stuffed olives
1 tbsp pinenuts
20 g/¾ oz/⅓ cup basil leaves
1–2 tbsp olive oil
Salt and pepper

tip
Sprouted seeds are not just for salads; they make a delicious and nutritious garnish for soups.

method
Preheat the oven to 180°C/350°F/Gas Mark 4.

Wash the carrots well. Peel, trim the ends, and cut into chunks. Peel the onion and discard the outer brown leaves. Cut into thin wedges. Place the carrots and onion in a roasting tray. Add the garlic cloves and orange peel. Scatter the coriander seeds on top and drizzle with olive oil. Bake for 40 minutes.

Meanwhile, boil the carrot and onion peels and trimmings in 1.5 litres/2¾ pints of water for 40 minutes.

At this point, you can prepare the sprouted seed pesto. Place all the ingredients except the olive oil into a food processor, and blend for a few seconds only. You still want the pesto to have texture. Spoon the mixture into a bowl, adjust the seasoning, and mix in the olive oil (1 or 2 tablespoons is a matter of taste; you decide). Leave the pesto covered until ready to eat.

By now, the carrots and stock should be ready. Season the roasted mixture well and leave to cool for 15 minutes. Strain the stock and leave it to cool as well. Discard the orange peel. Place the garlic cloves on a chopping board and press with the back of a spoon to extract the pulp. Add the pulp back to the stock. Place half of the roasted carrot mixture in the blender and add 500 ml/15 fl oz/1¾ cups of carrot stock. Blend until smooth, and pour directly into a sieve set on top of a large saucepan. Do the same with the other batch. Check if you need more or less stock each time. The consistency should be like that of double cream.

Reheat the soup gently, and serve with the sprouted seed pesto.

Harira

Serves 4–6
Preparation: 20 minutes
Cooking time: 1 hour 45 minutes
to make the stock,
40 minutes to cook

Harira is a traditional soup served in Morocco during the month of Ramadan to break the fast. It is also prepared for special occasions. There are many different versions of *harira*, and each region has its own. They all have lamb, lentils and spices in common. To serve its purpose, this soup has to be filling and nutritious. An egg can be added at the last minute. Some *harira* are thickened with a flour and water mixture called *tadouira*. I have eaten *harira* served with little lamb *keftas* on the side, and it was delicious.

ingredients

700 g/1 lb 9 oz lamb ribs
500 g/1 lb 2 oz chicken wings
2 tbsp ghee, or butter
1 tsp fresh thyme leaves, chopped
1 onion, finely chopped
1 celery stick, finely chopped
2 garlic cloves, crushed
1 tsp ground ginger
¼ tsp turmeric
Pinch of saffron
¼ tsp chilli powder
½ cinnamon stick
Salt and pepper
500 g/1 lb 2 oz tomatoes, peeled
(see p.142) and chopped
100 g/3½ oz/½ cup green lentils
50 g/2 oz/scant ¼ cup round rice
150 g/5 oz/½ cup cooked or tinned
chickpeas
1 lemon, quartered

Mint and coriander (cilantro) leaves,
to garnish

method

Preheat the oven to 220°C/425°F/Gas Mark 7.

Place the lamb ribs and chicken wings in a roasting dish and bake for 45 minutes.

Remove from the oven and place in a 3-litre soup pan. Add 200 ml/7 fl oz/¾ cup of water to the roasting dish and scrape away all the bits that have stuck to the bottom. Pour the juices into the soup pan. Add 1.4 litres/2½ pints of water, bring to a boil, reduce the heat and simmer, partly covered, for 1 hour.

Heat the ghee or butter and thyme leaves. Add the onion and celery and cook over a medium heat for 10 minutes, until soft and caramelized. Stir the onions from time to time to make sure they are not burning and reduce the heat if needed.

Meanwhile, remove the ribs and chicken from the stock. With two forks, scrape the meat off the bones and set aside, covered.

Add the garlic and spices to the onions and cook for 1 minute until well blended and the spices are fragrant. Add the tomatoes and cook for 5 minutes, until soft but still holding their shape.

Add the lentils and rice. Stir well, then add the lamb and chicken stock. Bring to a boil, and continue to boil for 5 minutes. Remove the foam from the surface. Reduce the heat and simmer for 20 minutes. Season well. Add the chickpeas and shredded meat, and simmer for 10 more minutes.

Serve the soup with a wedge of lemon, chopped mint and coriander.

Noodle soup, Japanese-style

Serves 4
Preparation: 10 minutes
+ overnight soaking
of the *kombu*
Cooking time: 20 minutes

The base of Japanese soups is a *dashi* stock made from *kombu* and *bonito* flakes. *Kombu* is a dried seaweed that has an incredibly high mineral and vitamin content. It is used in Japan to lower cholesterol and high blood pressure and ease digestion. *Kombu* is soaked overnight to release its flavour and goodness, then cooked with *bonito* flakes to make the first *dashi*. The first stock is more delicate and is reserved for clear soup eaten at the beginning of the meal. *Kombu* is cooked again with more *bonito* flakes to produce the second *dashi*. This stock is used for main-course soups and the famous *miso* soup. I have used the first *dashi* in this recipe for convenience. *Wakame* is also a seaweed (see p.19). You can find these ingredients in Japanese shops and some Chinese and Thai supermarkets. You can also buy instant *dashi*, but you won't get all the goodness that comes from soaking the *kombu*.

for the *dashi* stock
20 g/½ oz *kombu*
20 g/½ oz dried *bonito* flakes
+ 20 g/½ oz for the second stock

for the soup
2 tbsp mirin
2 tbsp *tamari* soy sauce
12 unpeeled king prawn tails (jumbo shrimp)
5–6 strands of *wakame*, cut into small pieces
200 g/7 oz buckwheat noodles
3 spring onions (scallions), finely sliced
4–6 tbsp radish sprouts

soy sauce and *shichimi* seven spice seasoning, to serve

tip
Kombu and *bonito* flakes make healthy cupboard staples, so stock up.

method

Make cuts in the *kombu* with scissors, being careful not to cut all the way through. *Kombu* becomes slimy when soaked and a large piece is easier to handle. Making the cuts helps release more nutrition and flavour. Do not wash *kombu* – the powder on the surface is a natural taste enhancer. Place the *kombu* in a bowl and cover with 1.5 litres/2¾ pints of water. Leave to soak overnight. The next day, bring the water to a boil. Just before it reaches boiling point, remove the *kombu* and set aside. Continue heating until the water reaches boiling point. Add the *bonito* flakes and turn off the heat. After all the flakes have sunk to the bottom, filter the stock through a sieve.

(While you are at it, you can make a second stock and freeze it for later. Place the *kombu* and *bonito* flakes in a 3-litre pot and cover with 1.5 litres/2¾ pints water. Bring to a light boil, add 20 g/½ oz of *bonito* flakes and turn off the heat. Wait until the flakes have sunk to the bottom, then pass the stock through a sieve.)

Bring the first *dashi* stock to a simmer and add the mirin and soy sauce. Add the prawns and simmer for 3 minutes. Add the *wakame*, and turn off the heat.

Meanwhile, cook the noodles in plenty of boiling water for 4 minutes. Drain and place into bowls. Pour the hot stock over the noodles, and serve garnished with chopped spring onions and red radish sprouts. Season to taste with extra soy sauce and *shichimi*, Japanese seven spice seasoning.

Mushroom & chestnut soup

Serves 4
Preparation: 15 minutes
Cooking time: 35 minutes
+ time to make the stock

With chestnuts and homemade chicken stock, this soup is not only delicious, it is also extremely nutritious. You can buy chestnuts that are already cooked and vacuum-packed. They are perfect for soups. The Parmesan crust gives a subtle and wonderful taste to the soup. You can serve the soup with grated Parmesan to bring out the taste even more.

ingredients

10 g/¼ oz dried porcini mushrooms
2 tbsp cooking olive oil
1 onion, finely chopped
500 g/1 lb 2 oz assorted mushrooms
    (chestnut [cremini], portobello,
    chanterelle), sliced
1 garlic clove, crushed
30 g/1 oz oats

1 x 200 g/7 oz pack whole chestnuts,
    roasted and ready to use
1 litre/1¾ pints/1 quart chicken stock
    or brown vegetable stock (see
    p.154 or p.159)
30 g/1 oz Parmesan crust
Salt and pepper

Grated Parmesan cheese, for garnish

method

Soak the dried mushrooms in 250 ml/8 fl oz/1 cup of water.

Heat the oil in a 3-litre pot. Add the onion, and cook for 2 minutes, until transparent and soft. Add the sliced fresh mushrooms, and stir-fry over high heat for 5 minutes, until the mushrooms are cooked and the juices have evaporated. Add the crushed garlic and oats. Stir-fry for 30 seconds more.

Add the soaked porcini mushrooms, their soaking juices, the chestnuts and the chicken stock. Bring to a boil, remove the scum that rises to the surface, reduce the heat and add the Parmesan crust. Let the soup simmer, partly covered, for 20 minutes.

Place about 350 ml/12 fl oz/1½ cups of the soup in a blender and process. Return the blended liquid into the soup. This will give some thickness to the soup without removing the lovely chunks of mushroom and chestnut to munch on.

Remove and discard the Parmesan crust — you might need two spoons, as it will be very soft and gooey. Adjust the seasoning, and serve the soup with extra grated Parmesan.

Lemongrass prawn broth with ginger prawn balls

Serves 4
Preparation: 15–20 minutes
Cooking time: 30 minutes

There is a real feel-good factor when you eat a Thai soup. It comes from the lightness of the stock and the clean, fresh flavours. There are a lot of steps for this recipe, but it is relatively simple to prepare. The most time-consuming step is shelling the prawns. I add watercress for an extra-healthy touch and because the peppery taste is a perfect complement.

ingredients
500 g/1 lb 2 oz whole raw tiger prawns (jumbo shrimp)

for the stock
2 tbsp sunflower oil
30 g/1 oz shallots, finely chopped
6 spring onions (scallions), sliced
1 celery stick, chopped
1 Thai chilli, slit open
2 lemongrass stalk, finely chopped
3 frozen lime leaves
Fish sauce, to season

for the prawn balls
Shelled tails from the prawns (shrimp), above
2 tsp grated ginger
3 spring onions (scallions)
the whites of 2 small eggs
1–1½ tbsp Thai fish sauce
½ Thai chilli, deseeded or not (to taste)

for the soup
1 tbsp sunflower oil
3 spring onions (scallions)
150 g/5 oz/1½ cups mangetout (snow peas)
50g/2 oz/⅔ cup watercress
Lime wedges, to serve

method
First, shell the prawns and reserve the heads and shells for the stock.

Heat the oil in a 3-litre pot. Add the shallots, spring onions, celery, chilli, lemongrass and lime leaves. Stir-fry for 2 minutes, until the vegetables are tender. Add the prawn heads and shells, and cook over medium heat for 5 minutes, until they are well coloured, stirring occasionally and making sure nothing burns at the bottom of the pot. Season well with fish sauce, which means 8–9 shakes of the bottle, and cover with 1.3 litres/2½ pints of water. Bring to a boil, remove the scum that rises to the surface, reduce the heat and simmer for 15–20 minutes.

Meanwhile, make the prawn balls. Place the prawn tails, ginger, spring onions, and egg whites in a food processor. Process until well blended. The mixture will be wet and very soft. Add the fish sauce and chopped chilli, and process again. Chilli without seeds will give a slight bite to the ginger balls. If you want them very spicy, keep the seeds. Using 2 spoons, form balls the size of chestnuts and place them on a plate. You should obtain 18–20 balls. By now, your stock will be ready.

Pass the stock through a strainer into a bowl and set aside.

For the soup, heat the oil in a 3-litre pot. Add the spring onions and mangetout, and stir-fry for 2 minutes. Add the stock and gently bring to a simmer. Add the prawn balls and simmer very gently for 4 minutes. If the liquid boils too much, the balls will split open. Add the watercress, and turn off the heat. Leave to infuse for a minute, then serve.

Chicken, tomato, garlic & ginger soup

Serves 4
Preparation: 10 minutes
+ 1 hour 30 minutes
to slow-cook the tomatoes
Cooking time: 25 minutes

In many cultures, chicken stock is used as a 'cure' for the common cold. So are ginger and garlic. This is why I have combined all these ingredients into a delicious tomato soup. This is my cure when I feel a cold coming on, and it has never let me down. Plenty of garlic and a good homemade chicken stock are crucial. I slow-cook the tomatoes so that the flavour is really concentrated. In addition to its medicinal qualities, it is a very delicious soup.

ingredients

1.5 kg/3 lb 6 oz tomatoes
Cloves from 1 large head of garlic
4 tbsp olive oil
1 large onion, finely sliced
1½ tbsp grated fresh ginger
½ tsp sugar
Salt and pepper
1.3 litres/2¼ pints chicken stock (see p.154)
150 g/5 oz sourdough bread, cut into 2½ cm/1 in pieces, or
80 g/2¾ oz vermicelli

method

Preheat the oven to 150°C/300°F/Gas Mark 2.

Halve the tomatoes. Remove the seeds with a teaspoon and place them in a bowl. Line a large oven tray with baking paper, and lay the tomatoes, cut face down, over the paper. Scatter the garlic cloves over the top and drizzle with olive oil. Place in the oven and cook for 1½ hours, until the tomatoes have shrivelled. Remove from the oven and leave to cool slightly.

Press the inside of the tomatoes through a sieve set over a bowl to remove as much juice as possible. Set aside.

Meanwhile, heat some olive oil in a 3-litre soup pan over medium heat, and cook the onion for 10–12 minutes until soft and caramelized. Add the ginger, and cook for another minute, until it starts sticking to the bottom of the pan. Add the strained juices from the tomatoes and stir well, scraping the bottom of the pan.

Using two forks, remove the skins from the tomatoes, they should come off easily. Place the tomatoes into the soup pan. Press on the garlic to pop out the mashed cloves and add them to the soup pan. Add any juices from the tray into the soup pan, and season. Add the chicken stock, bring to a simmer, and simmer for 15 minutes. If you are using vermicelli, add it 5 minutes before the end of the cooking time.

If you are using bread, preheat the grill and toast the bread on both sides until dry and golden. Divide the bread between the bowls, pour the soup over and serve.

“ Freeze a batch of this soup for that rainy day when you feel a cold coming on. ”

quick soups for one

Sometimes it is a bit complicated to cook a soup just for your own lunch. You need extra time to cook it the night before, or you might not have space in your freezer for the leftovers and you're afraid to waste part of it. This is why the soups in the rest of this chapter are designed for single portions, and some of them can be cooked in a jiffy.

Leek, red lentil, orange & spinach soup

Serves 1
Preparation: 5 minutes
Cooking time: 15 minutes

This delicious soup is so quick and simple it can be cooked just before going to work. Add pieces of pan-fried salmon and you have a full healthy meal.

ingredients

2 tsp olive oil
85 g/3 oz leek, finely sliced
½ tsp curry powder
30 g/1 oz/generous ⅛ cup red lentils
Juice of 1 large orange (100 ml/
3½ fl oz/scant ½ cup)
40 g/1½ oz/½ cup spinach

method

Heat the oil in a medium saucepan. Add the leek, and cook over medium heat for 3 minutes, stirring occasionally, until soft and just starting to caramelize.

Add the curry powder, and cook for a few seconds. Add the lentils, and stir until they are well coated with spices. Add 300 ml/½ pint/1¼ cups of water, cover and simmer for 5 minutes.

Add the orange juice and simmer, covered, for another 7 minutes. The soup should have a fairly thick consistency. Add the spinach, and cook for just one minute, until wilted.

That's it.

" Invest in a good quality Thermos™ flask to keep your soup piping hot until lunchtime. "

Pea, pinenut & watercress soup

Serves 1
Preparation: 5 minutes
Cooking time: 25 minutes

It is a known fact that frozen peas are often fresher and more packed with vitamins than peas in their pods which have been hanging around in shops for who knows how long. They are also a very convenient ingredient for stock.
I use an electric hand-held mixer to partly blend this soup. It is a very useful gadget to have. You can use it for most of the blended soups in this book.

ingredients

1 tsp cooking olive oil
15 g/½ oz shallots, finely chopped
1 small garlic clove, crushed
30 g/1 oz/¼ cup pinenuts
200 g/7 oz/2 cups garden peas, frozen
Salt and pepper
20 g/¾ oz/scant ⅓ cup watercress, roughly chopped

method

Heat the oil in a medium saucepan. Cook the shallots and garlic for 1–2 minutes, until they soften and start to caramelize. Add the pinenuts and cook for 1 minute, stirring constantly, until slightly golden. Add the frozen peas, and cook for 1 minute. Season, add 350 ml/12 fl oz/1½ cups of water, and bring to a boil. Reduce the heat, and simmer for 8 minutes.

Add the watercress, turn off the heat, and leave the soup to infuse and slightly cool for 10 minutes. Blend the soup roughly with an electric hand-held mixer, being careful not to splash yourself with hot liquid. The texture should be rough with bits of pinenut and peas to munch on. If you don't own a hand-held mixer, use a potato masher.

❝ You can use a handheld mixer for most of the blended soups in this book and save on the washing up. ❞

Cauliflower & green beans in spiced almond milk

Serves 1
Preparation: 10 minutes
Cooking time: 30 minutes

Almond milk is a wonderful alternative to dairy products. It is very nourishing and has a beautiful, subtle flavour. To speed up preparation of this soup, make the flavoured milk the day before.

ingredients

85 g/3 oz almonds
½ small onion, studded with a clove
1 spring onion (scallion), halved
1 small bay leaf
½ tsp mustard seeds
3 black peppercorns
2 tsp olive oil
½ garlic clove, crushed
100 g/3½ oz cauliflower, finely chopped
60 g/2½ oz green beans, topped and cut into 1 cm/½ in chunks

method

Heat a small frying pan and toast the almonds over medium heat for 5 minutes or until golden. Place in a blender and process with 400 ml/14 fl oz/1¾ cups of water until well blended. Pour directly into a sieve placed over a saucepan. Stir and press well to extract as much milk as possible. Reserve the almond paste. Add the onion, spring onion, bay leaf, mustard seeds and peppercorns to the almond milk. Bring to a boil, reduce the heat and simmer for 15 minutes.

Pass the flavoured milk through a fine sieve. Rinse the pan and return to the heat. Heat the oil, add the garlic, and cook for 30 seconds until slightly golden but not brown. Add the chopped vegetables. Stir-fry for about a minute, until the vegetables are well seasoned with the garlic oil. Add the spiced almond milk and bring to a boil. Reduce the heat and simmer for 10–12 minutes.

Leave to cool slightly, then whiz it for a few seconds with a hand-held blender. By blending some of the ingredients, you will enhance the taste and give the soup a silky, slightly thicker texture. Add a couple of tablespoons of almond paste, reheat gently and serve.

tip
You can use the leftover almond paste in other soups or even in cake mixtures.

Broccoli & fennel
with smoked mackerel

Serves 1
Preparation: 5 minutes
Cooking time: 20 minutes

Broccoli is the number one 'superfood' ingredient, so I had to have a broccoli soup in this section. To make it slightly unusual I have cooked it with fennel, as the two flavours really complement each other. I cook the florets separately, so they don't overcook in the soup and they keep their wonderful fresh taste. Served with smoked mackerel, it makes the perfect healthy lunch box.

ingredients
125 g/4 oz broccoli
2 tsp olive oil
½ small onion
85 g/3 oz fennel
½ tbsp Arborio rice

50 g/2 oz smoked flaked mackerel and
sourdough bread, to serve

method
Cut the florets of broccoli at their base and finely chop them. Set aside in a bowl. You should be left with the trunk of the broccoli. Remove some of the hard peel around the base and finely chop the centre.

Heat the oil in a 1-litre saucepan. Fry the onion, fennel and broccoli over medium heat for 3 minutes until soft and just starting to caramelize. Stir occasionally. Keep an eye on the fennel, as it is more starchy and will tend to stick to the bottom of the pan and burn. Add the rice and 350 ml/12 fl oz/1½ cups of water, bring to a boil and simmer gently, partly covered, for 20 minutes.

Meanwhile, bring a small saucepan of water to a boil. Add the chopped broccoli florets and cook for 1–2 minutes, or until tender. Strain and refresh under cold water to stop the cooking process.

Turn off the heat under the soup, and leave to cool for 10 minutes. Combine the soup and the broccoli florets in a blender and process until smooth.

Pour the soup into the saucepan and reheat gently. Serve the soup with flakes of mackerel and sourdough bread.

Quinoa & vegetables with preserved lemon

Serves 1
Preparation: 10 minutes
Cooking time: 15 minutes

Quinoa is usually considered a grain, but it is actually the seeds of a leafy vegetable from the spinach family, originally from South America, where it has been consumed for more than 5,000 years. It has an interesting texture. It is soft and creamy, with a slightly crunchy centre. Because of its high protein content, quinoa has become extremely popular worldwide and is now easy to find in health-food shops and even supermarkets. I have used preserved lemons in this recipe. They are whole lemons preserved in salt. You can find them in speciality delis and Middle Eastern shops. They are wonderful in soups.

ingredients

1 tsp olive oil
100 g/3½ oz/2 cups chestnut (cremini) mushrooms, chopped
¼ tsp coriander seeds, crushed
85 g/3 oz leeks, sliced
½ tsp ground ginger
½ tsp tomato paste
1 tbsp quinoa
50 g/2 oz soya beans, fresh or frozen
Salt and pepper
1 tsp preserved lemon, chopped

method

Heat the oil in a saucepan, and fry the mushrooms for 2 minutes. Add the coriander seeds, and cook for a few seconds. Add the leek slices and the ground ginger, and cook for 2 more minutes. Add the tomato paste, and cook for a few seconds.

Add the quinoa and soya beans. Season well with salt and pepper, and stir until well coated with the juice and spices. Add 350 ml/12 fl oz/1½ cups of water and the preserved lemon. Bring to a boil, reduce the heat and simmer, covered, for 15 minutes.

" If you can't find preserved lemons, simply flavour this soup with a squeeze of fresh lemon. "

Spinach & fenugreek
with goat's cheese toasts

Serves 1
Preparation: 10 minutes
Cooking time: 10 minutes

Fenugreek has been used as a medicinal herb for centuries. It originated in the Mediterranean. Hippocrates already considered it as a soothing remedy. From there, it spread to India. In Ayurvedic medicine, it is used to help clear accumulated toxins in the body, improve flatulence and poor digestion. In the UK, fenugreek seeds are widely available, but fenugreek leaves are found mainly in Indian grocery stores. They are slightly bitter with a curry aftertaste, which is perfect with spinach. The flavour of this soup goes really well with fresh goat's cheese. Serve it in the soup or on the side, spread on toasted slices of bread.

ingredients

125 g/4 oz/1⅓ cups baby spinach, washed
2 tsp olive oil
½ small onion, finely chopped
1 small garlic clove, crushed
½ tsp ginger, grated
¼ tsp fenugreek seeds
½ tsp ground cumin
1 small tomato, peeled and chopped
¼ tsp tomato paste (optional)
Salt and pepper
Small pinch of chilli powder
1 tbsp fresh fenugreek leaves, chopped (optional)

Fresh goat's cheese and toasted slices of baguette, to serve

method

Bring 350 ml/12 fl oz/1½ cups of water to a boil. Add the spinach, and cook for 1 minute, then remove from the water with a slotted spoon and leave aside to drain. Reserve the spinach stock. When cool enough to handle, finely chop the spinach.

Heat the oil in a 1-litre saucepan, and fry the onion for 3 minutes, until soft and starting to brown slightly. Add the garlic and ginger, and cook for 1 minute, until slightly golden. Add the spices, and cook for 1 minute, until fragrant. Add the chopped tomato and tomato paste, if using, and cook for 3 minutes. Add the spinach, and stir until well coated with the spice and tomato mix. Season well, and add the chilli powder (add extra chilli powder if you want it extra spicy). Add the spinach stock, cover and simmer for 5 minutes.

Add the chopped fresh fenugreek leaves, if using, and turn off the heat. Allow to cool for 10 minutes, then partly blend the soup using a hand-held mixer. You want some bits of spinach to remain.

This soup is delicious served with baked slices of baguette spread with fresh goat's cheese. You can serve these toasts warm. Place them under the grill until melted and golden.

Red pepper, red cabbage & saffron soup

Serves 1
Preparation: 15 minutes
Cooking time: 30 minutes

Combine red peppers and red cabbage: you have the ultimate antioxidant combination and the taste is wonderful. I have tried many different ways to cook red cabbage and I was never thrilled about the results until I found out that it doesn't need to cook for very long, or it becomes bland. In this recipe, it is quickly pan-fried, then added to the soup for just a few minutes.

ingredients

2½ tsp olive oil
½ red onion, finely sliced
85 g/3 oz red (bell) peppers, deseeded and finely sliced or shredded
50 g/2 oz orange (bell) peppers, deseeded and finely sliced or shredded
1 small garlic clove, crushed
Small pinch of saffron
125 g/4 oz red cabbage
50 ml/2 fl oz/scant ¼ cup freshly squeezed orange juice
½ tsp sugar
Chilli sauce, to serve (optional)

method

Heat 2 tsp of the oil in a 2-litre pot, add the very finely sliced onion and the peppers, and cook for 10 minutes, until caramelized. Add the garlic and saffron, and cook for 30 seconds. Add 350 ml/12 fl oz/1½ cups of water, bring to a boil, reduce the heat and simmer, covered, for 15 minutes.

Meanwhile, finely slice the red cabbage. Heat the rest of the oil in a small frying pan. Add the cabbage and stir-fry for 2 minutes. Add the orange juice and sugar. Cook for 3–4 minutes, until the cabbage starts to soften. Add to the soup and cook for 3 more minutes. Serve as it is or with 2–3 shakes of chilli sauce.

chilled & cool

Chilled soups are not just for warm summer evenings;
they will also add a bit of intrigue to a dinner party.
They can be used as *amuse-bouches* (mouth-teasers),
to keep your taste buds entertained until dinner arrives
on the table. And shot glasses of your favourite chilled
soup served with an aperitif are definitely healthier
than crisps and peanuts.

As I mention in the Q&A section, you tend to eat less of a
cold soup, so portion sizes in most of these recipes are
smaller. There are a few exceptions, such as the soups
designed for picnics or for reheating.

I have combined healthier alternatives to the usual
creamy chilled soups. Only three of the soups in this
chapter contain cream. Even my twist on vichyssoise
with sweet potatoes and leeks is cream-free.

And if chilled soups give you goose bumps, you will find
that the smooth courgette and turmeric, the cream of
mussel with lime leaves and the dairy-free sweet potato
vichyssoise are all equally delicious warmed up.

Crisp radish & yoghurt with sesame oil

Serves 4–6
(8–10 tapas servings)
Preparation: 15 minutes
No cooking

Use pink round radishes for this soup. They should be shiny with no blemishes. Don't throw away the tops – keep them wrapped in wet kitchen roll inside a plastic bag; they can be used in the Asparagus and radish top soup (p.15). It is best to prepare the soup at the last minute or the yoghurt will slightly separate and lose its creaminess.

ingredients

500 g/1 lb 2 oz radishes, grated
1 large spring onion (scallion), roughly chopped
500 g/1 lb 2 oz yoghurt
Salt and freshly ground black pepper
2 tsp honey
2 tsp toasted sesame oil

2 tsp toasted sesame seeds, or toasted assorted seeds, to garnish

method

First, make the yoghurt base: place half of the radishes, the chopped spring onion and half the yoghurt in a food processor and blend until smooth. Transfer the mixture into a bowl and season with the salt and pepper, honey and sesame oil. Taste the mixture and adjust the seasoning. You might like it sweeter or with more sesame oil. In any case, this base should be well seasoned because, once more yoghurt and radishes are added, it shouldn't be over-mixed.

Finely shred the rest of the radishes. (You can prepare the base and shred the radishes in advance and keep everything refrigerated until ready to serve.)

Just before serving the soup, taste the base and season it again if needed. Gently add the remaining yoghurt and the shredded radishes. Do not over-mix, or the yoghurt will separate, and you want a thick, creamy consistency. Spoon the mixture into small dishes or cups, sprinkle the top with seeds, and serve.

" This makes an ideal palate cooler after a spicy dish. "

Smooth courgette & turmeric soup

Serves 4-6 generously
(12-14 tapas servings)
Preparation: 10 minutes
Cooking time: 45 minutes
+ a couple of hours to chill

ingredients

2 tbsp vegetable oil
600 g/1 lb 5 oz courgette (zucchini), diced
1 onion, diced
1 tsp sugar
Salt to taste
15 g/½ oz ginger, finely chopped
1 tsp mustard seeds
1½ tsp coriander seeds
1 tsp turmeric
25 g/1 oz/⅛ cup basmati rice

Yoghurt and lemon, to garnish

Make this soup in the summer months, when courgettes are at their best. The turmeric gives a slight bitterness that really complements the courgette. It is a lovely soup for picnics and can be made the day before. It is also delicious served warm.

method

Heat the oil in a 3-litre soup pan. Add the chopped onion and courgette. Cook over medium heat for 10 minutes, stirring occasionally. You don't want the bottom of the pan to burn, but you want the excess water from the courgette to evaporate. Add the sugar and salt. Cook for 1 minute. Add the chopped ginger, spices and rice and cook for another minute to release the aroma from the spices. Add 1.2 litres/2¼ pints of water, bring to a boil, and simmer partly covered for 30 minutes. I usually balance the lid so that about 5 cm/2 in of the soup is uncovered and some liquid can evaporate. This will help concentrate the flavours.

Leave to cool down for 20 minutes and then whiz in a blender in 3 batches until smooth. Leave to chill in the fridge for a couple of hours, or 1 hour on ice, until ready to serve. It is delicious on its own or with a dollop of yoghurt or a squeeze of lemon.

tip

Always let your soup cool down for at least 15 minutes before putting in a blender. The high heat will create pressure and the cover of the blender might pop off while the motor is running! Half-fill your blender and blend in batches.

66 *Also good served warm on chilly summer nights.* 99

Exotic citrus soup

Serves 4-6
(8-10 tapas servings)
Preparation: 15 minutes
Cooking time: 10 minutes
+ 30 minutes to chill

Perfect for a hot summer night while you wait for the fish or chicken to finish cooking on the barbecue. This pungent soup is also good as a palate cleanser between dishes. I have used agar flakes just to give the soup a slight jellied consistency.

ingredients

2 grapefruit
3 oranges
1 large lime
1 tsp grated ginger
1 Thai green chilli, whole
1 tbsp sugar
400 ml/14 fl oz/1¾ cups water
1 tbsp agar flakes
1 tbsp tamari soy sauce

method

Remove the zest, pith and skin of each citrus fruit following the curve of the fruit. You need a very sharp or serrated knife to do this. Then holding the fruit in one hand, slide the knife down one side of a segment, then the other side. Remove the flesh of each segment in this way and place into a saucepan. When all the segments have been cut, squeeze the remaining pith with your hands to extract as much juice as you can. Add the lime zest, the grated ginger, chilli, sugar and water to the saucepan. Add the agar flakes and stir well. Simmer gently for 5 minutes. The citrus segments will start to break. Don't stir the soup too much because you want some segments to remain whole.

Leave to cool, then season with the tamari sauce. You can remove the chilli at this point, or leave it in if you want a spicy soup. Chill it in the fridge for at least an hour, or overnight, or on ice as below.

tip

Mix 1 kg/2¼ lb of ice with a couple of handfuls of rock salt and 500 ml/ 18 fl oz/2 cups of water in a bowl. The salt will melt the ice quickly, and the temperature of the water will drop suddenly. Place your cooled soup container into the iced water. This is the quickest way to chill your soup – it should take only 30 minutes.

Creamy cucumber soup with spring onion & basil

Serves 4-6
(8-10 tapas servings)
Preparation: 10 minutes
Cooking time: 7 minutes

Easy and quick to prepare, cold cucumber soup is perfect for an improvised starter. I like it flavoured with basil, but you can also use a mixture of chervil, tarragon and dill to vary the taste. I prefer Persian cucumbers, which are smaller and thinner than the traditional cucumbers found in supermarkets; they are full of flavour and rarely bitter.

ingredients

1 tbsp olive oil
450 g/1 lb spring onions (scallions), cleaned and chopped
Salt and pepper
500 ml/18 fl oz/2 cups milk
750 g/1 lb 11 oz Persian cucumbers, or 2 large cucumbers, peeled and roughly chopped
50 g/2 oz/generous ¾ cup basil leaves, chopped
100 ml/3½ fl oz/scant ½ cup double (heavy) cream

Small basil leaves, to garnish

method

Spring onions, like leeks, can contain dirt inside their green tops. Slice the top green part with a knife lengthwise and clean them well under running water. Discard the root and chop the white and green parts into small slices.

Heat the oil in a medium frying pan. Fry the spring onion slices for 1–2 minutes, until just wilted. Season well, add the milk and bring to a simmer for 3 minutes. Remove from the heat and leave to cool.

Place half of the spring onion mixture in a blender. Add half the cucumber and basil and whiz until smooth. Pass through a sieve set over a bowl. Repeat with the other half.

Add the cream, mix well and place on ice for 1 hour to chill. Serve garnished with small basil leaves.

Beetroot, goat's yoghurt & coriander soup

Serves 4-6
(8-10 tapas servings)
Preparation: 10 minutes
Cooking time: 1 hour
+ 1 hour to cool (if you are
baking the beetroot)

Beetroot is a magical vegetable for soups. It is equally delicious in cold or hot soups. I would highly recommend baking the beetroot yourself for this recipe, but if you don't have time, make sure to buy plain beetroot, not the ones marinated in vinegar. I like to serve this soup with toasted bread rubbed with fresh garlic and brushed with olive oil. Don't hesitate to toast your bread slices on the side of the barbecue if you've got one going. There is nothing like barbecue-toasted bread.

ingredients

600 g/1 lb 5 oz beetroot (beet),
peeled and quartered
3 unpeeled garlic cloves
Salt and pepper
1 tbsp olive oil
450 g/1 lb goat's milk yoghurt
1 small bunch fresh coriander
(cilantro), roughly chopped
Green chilli sauce, or green tabasco

for the garnish

4 slices of sourdough bread
1 large garlic clove
A few drizzles of extra-virgin olive oil

method

Preheat the oven to 200°C/400°F/Gas Mark 6.

Place a large sheet of parchment paper over a similar sized sheet of foil, then place the beetroot over one half, add the garlic cloves, season and drizzle with the olive oil. Fold the parchment and foil over the top and tuck the edges of foil together to tightly close the parcel. This way, the beetroot will bake in their own steam and will not dry out. Bake for 50 minutes. Remove from the oven and leave to cool in the foil parcel for at least 1 hour.

When cool enough to handle, finely chop the beetroot. Season well with salt and pepper, and leave to rest for a few minutes to dissolve the salt crystals. Place half of the beetroot in the blender with half the goat's yoghurt, half the coriander and 300 ml/½ pint water. Process until smooth. Pour into a bowl and proceed with the other half of the ingredients and the same amount of water. Adjust the seasoning and consistency. Add a bit more water if needed. Add 6–7 shakes of green chilli sauce and stir well.

The soup will have a slightly grainy texture. You can pass it through a fine sieve and your soup will be very smooth. Quickly chill on ice, or chill in the fridge for a couple of hours.

Just before serving, toast the bread or place it on the side of the barbecue where the coals are not fierce. Watch the bread, as it will toast very quickly. Prick the garlic cloves with the fork and rub them on the toasted bread. Drizzle each slice with olive oil and serve with the soup.

Velvet melon with green peppercorns & Serrano crisps

Serves 4-6 generously
(12-14 tapas servings)
Preparation: 15 minutes
Cooking time: 15 minutes for
the ham crisps

Melon gazpacho is extremely refreshing as a summer starter. I have used cantaloupe orange-fleshed melon for this recipe, but you can use honeydew or '*piel de sapo*'. The green peppercorn gives a real bite to this gazpacho. If you can find fresh Thai peppercorn, the taste will be even more intense and flowery. The Serrano ham crisps are baked in the oven to give a real crispiness and a more intense taste. You can crisp Parma ham or pancetta in the same way.

ingredients

25 g/1 oz breadcrumbs
½ tsp sherry vinegar
2 large cantaloupe melons
Salt to taste
½–1 tsp fresh or preserved Thai
green peppercorns, crushed
2 tbsp extra-virgin olive oil
8 slices Serrano ham

method

Preheat the oven to 200°C/400°F/Gas Mark 6.

Place the breadcrumbs in a small bowl. Add 60 ml/2 fl oz/4 tbsp of water and the vinegar, and leave to soak while you chop the melons.

Halve the melons and spoon out the seeds. Cut into wedges and run the knife along the peel to remove it. Chop the flesh.

Place half the melon cubes, the soaked breadcrumbs and 60 ml/2 fl oz/4 tbsp more water in the blender. Process until smooth. Add the crushed peppercorns and half the olive oil, and process again for about 10 seconds. The olive oil gives a velvety texture and beautiful golden tone to the soup. Transfer to a bowl. Proceed in the same way with the second batch. Chill on ice.

Spread the Serrano ham slices on a baking tray lined with baking paper. Bake for 12–15 minutes, until slightly dark in colour without burning. Remove from the oven and leave to cool. The ham will become really crisp as it cools.

Pour the soup into bowls or glasses, and garnish with Serrano ham crisps on the side.

" If you don't want to bake the ham crisps, you can simply garnish with thin strips of Serrano ham. "

Cream of mussel with fennel & lime leaves

Serves 4–6 generously
(12–14 tapas servings)
Preparation: 25 minutes
+ 1 hour to soak
Cooking time: 30 minutes
+ 1 hour to chill

Lime leaves give a beautiful aroma to fish and shellfish soups. You can buy a bag of frozen lime leaves in some Oriental grocery stores and keep it in the freezer. You don't even need to defrost them; just add them frozen to the simmering stock. Mussels can store a lot of grit. If you soak them in clear water for an hour, they will partly purge themselves. Renew the water two or three times.

ingredients

1.3 kg/3 lb mussels
2 tbsp olive oil
450 g/1 lb fennel, cubed
1 onion, finely chopped
5 frozen lime leaves

(Pictured on p.105)

tip

To clean mussels, scrub the shells under cold running water. Remove the 'beard' hanging from the side by pulling firmly towards the round edge of the shell. If you pull in the other direction, it will be harder and you will tear the mussel inside. If a mussel is opened, lightly press on it to close it. If it stays closed, it means it is still alive and you can use it. If it reopens, discard it.

method

Soak the mussels for 1 hour, then clean them (see Tip). Heat a large pot with a tight-fitting lid. When hot, add the mussels and cover. After a couple of minutes, shake the pot and check that the mussels are starting to open up. Cook for 2 more minutes and then turn off the heat. Leave aside for a couple more minutes; they will finish cooking in their own steam. When they have all opened, the juices released (about 400 ml/14 fl oz/1¾ cups) will be the base of your soup stock.

Heat the oil in a 3-litre soup pan. Add the fennel and chopped onion and cook over a medium-low heat for 10 minutes, stirring occasionally. They should become soft, but not caramelized.

Meanwhile, shell the mussels and place them in a bowl. Reserve a dozen on the half-shell for garnish. Filter the stock from all impurities by running it through a very fine sieve or lining your sieve with a square of muslin.

Add the stock to the fennel and onion mixture, along with 750 ml/1½ pints of water. Bring to a boil, add 3 of the lime leaves, and simmer for 15–20 minutes. Two minutes before the end of the cooking time, add the shelled mussels to the soup. Turn off the heat, add the rest of the lime leaves, and leave to cool for 15 minutes.

Pour one-third of the soup into a blender and process until smooth. Proceed the same way for the rest of the soup. Pass through a fine sieve set over the soup pan. Chill for at least 1 hour.

Serve, garnished with the reserved mussels.

Mixed nut *ajo blanco*

Serves 4–6
(8–10 tapas servings)
Preparation: 5 minutes
Cooking time: 50 minutes
(including cooling time)
+ 30 minutes to chill on ice

Ajo blanco is a famous white gazpacho from Andalucía made with almonds and garlic and eaten well-chilled with ripe, sweet Muscatel grapes. Every year for the past 40 years, on the first Saturday of September, 3,000 litres of this white nectar are produced for the '*Fiesta del Ajo Blanco*' in the province of Malaga. This festival is all about local tradition, open-air museums, flamenco and, of course, a free tasting of this delicious soup. In Andalucía, *ajo blanco* is made with almonds, but I have used an assortment of nuts, which gives it a more complex and richer taste. Muscatel grapes are perfect as a garnish. I also like it garnished with very ripe dark red pomegranate seeds.

ingredients
200 g/7 oz ciabatta loaf, crust removed
100 g/3½ oz/⅔ cup cashew nuts
100 g/3½ oz/⅔ cup almonds
40 g/1½ oz/scant ⅓ cup pinenuts
15 g/½ oz garlic cloves
Salt and pepper
1 tbsp sherry vinegar
2 tbsp olive oil

Muscatel grapes and/or pomegranate seeds, for garnish

method
Preheat the oven to 180ºC/350ºF/Gas Mark 4. Soak the bread in 300 ml/½ pint of water.

Place the nuts on a baking tray lined with parchment paper. Bake for 15 minutes and then leave to cool for 30 minutes.

Peel the garlic cloves. Halve them, and remove any green germ from the centre. This will make the soup easier to digest. Place the garlic in a pestle and mortar, add a large pinch of salt, and crush until you obtain a paste.

Place half of the cooled nuts, garlic paste, plus 225 ml/8 fl oz/1 cup of water in a blender. Process until smooth. Add half of the sherry vinegar and the olive oil and blend again. Transfer into a bowl and repeat with the other half of the ingredients and the same amount of water. Check the seasoning again.

Chill on ice for 30 minutes. Serve well chilled, with Muscatel grapes or pomegranate seeds to garnish.

66 Roasting nuts in the oven first will boost their flavour. 99

Cream of aubergine with garlic & anchovies

Serves 4–6
(8–10 tapas servings)
Preparation: 5 minutes
Cooking time: 1 hour
+ 20 minutes (includes cooling time)

This soup is inspired by the taste of *bagna cauda*, a warm anchovy and garlic dip served with *crudités* in Piedmont and Provence. I have used baked aubergine to give a Moorish taste to the soup, and roasted garlic rather than raw garlic for a more subtle flavour. Make sure you buy good-quality Spanish anchovies in olive oil. If not, you will have to use more anchovies and the soup will become too salty. It is a rich soup and is best served in small quantities. I love the crunchiness and peppery taste of radishes with this soup.

ingredients

1 kg/2¼ lb aubergines (eggplants)
The cloves of 1 large garlic head, unpeeled
1 small lemon, quartered
Large pinch of salt
1 tsp sugar
1 tbsp + 100 ml/3½ fl oz/scant ½ cup olive oil
100 ml/3½ fl oz/scant ½ cup single (light) cream
6–10 anchovy fillets
Salt and pepper

1 bunch of radishes, to serve

method

Preheat the oven to 180°C/350°F/Gas Mark 4.

Halve the aubergines and score the skin with a knife, so that the heat will penetrate more easily and they will cook quicker. Place the aubergine, garlic cloves and lemon slices on a baking tray. Sprinkle with salt and sugar and drizzle with olive oil. Bake for 50–55 minutes.

Remove the tray from the oven and leave to cool for 20 minutes. Scrape the aubergine flesh and place directly into a blender. Squeeze the garlic pulp out of its skin by pressing on the cloves with a spoon. Place in the blender. Scrape the pulp from the lemon directly over the blender, so you don't lose any juice. Add 600 ml/1 pint of water and process until smooth. Add the olive oil and cream, and process again. This will emulsify the soup and give it a creamy consistency. Progressively add the anchovy fillets, blending after each addition, until the taste is to your liking. This soup doesn't need to be chilled; it is nice served at room temperature. By the time you've made it, it will be ready to serve. Adjust the seasoning and serve with radishes.

" A small portion of this soup would fit beautifully into a tapas menu. "

Vodka gazpacho

Serves 4-6 generously
(12-14 tapas servings)
Preparation: 25 minutes
(no cooking)
+ 30 minutes to chill on ice

A good friend of mine, Sergio, who is Italian and a fantastic cook, always adds a splash of vodka at the end of cooking his risotto to bring out the flavours. For years, I thought he was joking, until I tried it myself, and I must admit that, used in small quantities, it is a fantastic taste enhancer. You can simply enhance the taste of this gazpacho or you can turn it into a Bloody Mary gazpacho, letting your guests help themselves to the vodka. Either way, it is a fun gazpacho for picnics.

ingredients

50 g/2 oz/1 cup fresh breadcrumbs
1 tsp sherry vinegar
1 kg/2¼ lb ripe tomatoes, chopped
2 medium green (bell) peppers, deseeded and chopped
2 Romano red peppers, deseeded and chopped
100 g/3½ oz/⅔ cup sweet white onions, chopped
Salt and freshly ground pepper
3 tbsp extra-virgin olive oil
Tabasco sauce
3 tbsp vodka
1 cucumber, peeled and cut into 10 cm/4 in strips, to garnish

method

Place the breadcrumbs in a small bowl. Pour 50 ml/2 fl oz/4 tbsp of water and the vinegar on top. Leave to soak while you chop the vegetables.

You will need to do the blending in 3 batches. Place a third of the tomatoes, green and red peppers, onion and soaked breadcrumbs in a blender and process until smooth. The tomatoes should give enough juice, but you can always add a bit of water if you think the mixture is too thick. Transfer the mixture into a bowl. Proceed in the same way for each remaining third.

Pass the gazpacho mixture through a sieve, to remove the tomato and pepper skins. Transfer the sieved mixture back into the blender. Season. Add the olive oil, a few shakes of Tabasco and vodka, and blend for a few seconds. Again, do it in batches, if needed.

Chill on ice, or for 3 hours in the fridge. Serve in glasses, with extra vodka and Tabasco nearby.

Dairy-free sweet potato vichyssoise

Serves 4-6 generously
(12-14 tapas servings)
Preparation: 10 minutes
Cooking time: 40 minutes
+ 1 hour to chill

There are many stories about where and when vichyssoise was invented. My favourite links it to the Ritz-Carlton in the twenties, during one of those stifling hot New York summers. Louis Diat, the chef at the time, had made an enormous batch of leek and potato soup that he didn't dare serve on such a sticky, hot night. Leaning over his chilled batch of soup, he had the brilliant idea to mix it with cream and give it the catchy name of 'vichyssoise', which has since become the most popular chilled soup in the world. Thinking of people with lactose intolerance, I have concocted an unusual version of vichyssoise which tastes wonderful and is completely dairy-free.

ingredients

300 g/11 oz leeks
450 g/1 lb sweet potatoes
2 tbsp olive oil
1.2 litres/2 pints green vegetable stock (p.160)
4 tbsp oat cream
Salt and pepper
Freshly grated nutmeg

About 2 tbsp finely chopped chives, for garnish

method

Slice the top green part of the leeks in half lengthwise and run under cold water to remove all traces of dirt. Discard the roots and thinly slice. Peel the sweet potatoes and cut into cubes.

Heat the oil in a 3-litre soup pan. Add the leeks and sweet potatoes. Cook for 10 minutes over a medium heat, stirring occasionally. The vegetables should be slightly golden, but mustn't burn.

Add the stock and oat cream, bring to a boil and simmer for 20 minutes. Remove from the heat and leave to cool for 10 minutes.

Place a third of the soup in a blender. Process until smooth and pour into a bowl. Do the same with each remaining third. Season with salt, freshly grated nutmeg and black peppercorn. Chill on ice for at least 1 hour.

Serve, garnished with finely chopped chives.

" Grownups like this cool; kids like it hot. "

Summer vegetables in lemongrass stock

Serves 4–6
Preparation: 15 minutes
Cooking time: 20 minutes
+ 1 hour to chill on ice

The principle of this soup is to use summer vegetables at their freshest and to keep them crunchy to seal that freshness. It is an ideal soup if you grow your own or are just back from a pick-your-own trip. The stock can be made as and when you prepare the soup by just throwing the vegetable trimmings into a pot of simmering water. I have added lemongrass and lime to give the stock a real kick. You can also add a hint of mint or tarragon – but just a hint, don't overpower the stock. *Nuoc nam* is a Vietnamese fish sauce and seasoning that I find more delicate than Thai fish sauce. You can find it in Oriental and Vietnamese grocery shops. You can use it as the final seasoning.

ingredients

200 g/7 oz/2 cups podded broad (fava) beans
225 g/8 oz courgettes (zucchini)
125 g/4 oz baby asparagus, or thin French (green) beans
5 spring onions (scallions), cleaned and chopped
3 lemongrass, slit in half lengthwise and chopped
Zest of 2 limes
Salt and pepper

A dash of *nuoc nam*, and wedges of lime, to serve

method

Bring 1.3 litres/2¼ pints of water to a boil in a 2-litre soup pan. Add the broad beans and cook for 1 minute, or until they all rise to the surface. Remove the beans with a slotted spoon and cool them under cold running water. Keep the water in the pan simmering, as you will use it to make the stock.

Skin the broad beans by making a slit along each bean with the nail of your thumb, then popping the bean out. Place the beans in a large bowl and set aside. Return the skins to the pan of simmering water.

Trim the courgettes and add the trimmings to the simmering water. Finely chop the rest and add to the bowl of broad beans.

Trim the asparagus and add the trimmings to the water. Chop the rest and add to the bowl with the broad beans and courgettes.

Add the chopped spring onion, lemongrass and lime zest to the vegetable stock. Continue to simmer, covered, for 15 minutes. Strain the stock and return it to the soup pan. Season well and bring back to a simmer. Add the vegetables and cook for 3 minutes. They should still be crunchy. Transfer the soup to a bowl and chill over iced water. This will keep the vegetables looking green and fresh.

Serve chilled with a dash of Vietnamese *nuoc nam* and a wedge of lime.

Mexican cream of avocado

Serves 4–6
(8–10 tapas servings)
Preparation: 1 hour if you are
making stock; 5 minutes if
you already have stock
Cooking time: 5 minutes
+ 20 minutes to cool

ingredients

4 avocados (about 225 g/8 oz each)
Juice of 2 limes
1 litre/1¾ pints chicken stock, or
vegetable stock
4–8 slices of jalapeño chilli in vinegar
4 tbsp sour cream

Red onion, thinly sliced, and extra
jalapeños, to serve

Jalisco is a province on the west coast of Mexico which specializes in growing avocados. This soup is inspired by the avocado soup served in the area. It is traditionally made with chicken stock, but is also delicious (and lighter) made with green vegetable stock (p.160). This is a rich soup and should be served in small portions.

method

If you have just made chicken or vegetable stock, allow it to cool to room temperature. If you are using chilled stock out of the fridge, warm it up slightly.

Halve the avocados, remove the stone and spoon the flesh into a bowl. Pour the juice of 1½ limes over the top and mash with a fork. Place half the mashed avocado and 400 ml/14 fl oz of the stock in a blender and process until smooth. Add half the jalapeño slices, half the sour cream and a bit more stock, if needed. Repeat with the other half of the ingredients.

The degree of ripeness of the avocados will have an effect on the texture of the soup, so add the stock progressively and check as you go. The consistency of the soup should be like double cream.

Chill the soup rapidly over ice for 20 minutes and serve with thin slivers of red onion and the extra jalapeños.

" Avocados oxidize quickly. This soup should ideally be made no longer than about 30 minutes before serving. "

Tomato & gooseberry soup with herb chantilly

Serves 4–6
(8–10 tapas servings)
Preparation: 10 minutes
Cooking time: 30 minutes

Tomato being a fruit, it really lends itself to both savoury and sweet flavours. The gooseberries add a real floral touch to the tomato taste. Gooseberry season is short, but they freeze well and some garden centre food shops stock them. The herb chantilly is best prepared at the last minute. It also makes a lovely garnish for any root vegetable soups such as carrot, parsnip or celeriac.

ingredients
350 g/12 oz/2⅓ cups gooseberries
100 g/3½ oz/½ cup sugar
900 g/2 lb tomatoes,
very ripe and roughly chopped
Salt and freshly ground white pepper

for the herb chantilly
200 ml/7 fl oz/generous ¾ cup
whipping cream
2 tbsp tarragon, chopped
2 tbsp coriander (cilantro), chopped
2 tbsp chives, chopped
2 tsp grain mustard
Salt and freshly ground pepper

(Pictured on p.105)

method
Place the gooseberries in a saucepan with 200 ml/7 fl oz/generous ¾ cup of water and the sugar. Cover and simmer slowly for 10 minutes, until the gooseberries are mushy.

Mix a third of the chopped tomatoes with a third of the gooseberry compote in a blender and process until smooth. Pour directly into a sieve set on top of a bowl. Proceed in the same way for each remaining third.

Using a large spoon, stir and push the mixture through the sieve to extract as much juice as possible. Season with salt and freshly ground white pepper. Leave aside to cool. You don't want the soup to be very cold; it should be at room temperature.

Just before serving, prepare the herb chantilly. Whip the cream until it starts to set. Add the chopped herbs, mustard and seasoning. Mix gently, being careful not to overwork the cream, which might become hard and lose its unctuousness.

Serve the soup with a dollop of herb chantilly.

tip
Keep the cream, bowl and whisk cold in the fridge; the colder they all are, the easier the cream will be to whip.

play posh

The seventies saw the creation of 'nouvelle cuisine', with an emphasis on presentation, minimalist portions, and a healthier way to cook and eat. Today, chefs have gone one step further and turned their kitchens into laboratories in search of new ways to thrill. New flavours and textures have emerged through the use of syringes, vacuum cooking, pressured siphons and smoking guns. There are two ways to play posh. One is to replace your food processor with a 'rotary evaporator' to extract the flavour of your soup; the other is simply to be clever with presentation and flavours.

To be clever with flavours means buying top-quality ingredients. Finnan haddock, which is dried and smoked on the bone, tastes very different from a smoked fillet of haddock you might buy in a plastic container in your local supermarket. A stock made with Jabugo ham bone will be richer, almost sweeter, than one made with any old cured ham bone. There is also a big difference between vanilla pods, depending on where they come from. Corn kernels cut off the cob will taste fresher and more perfumed than will tinned corn, which is likely to transmit a metallic taste to your soup. Cherry tomatoes are more concentrated in flavour than regular tomatoes.

There is nothing complicated or impossible to make in this section. For example, the milk foam that tops the cappuccino of mushrooms would probably come out of a siphon in a professional kitchen, but I have made a simplified version so that you can obtain a similar result without investing in any special gadgets.

Cappuccino of mushrooms with truffle oil foam

Makes 6 cup servings
Preparation: 10 minutes
+ 1 hour to make the stock
Cooking time: 20 minutes

Cappuccino of mushrooms is now a standard on posh restaurant menus, so I just had to include a recipe in this section. It is literally done as a cappuccino. If you own a cappuccino machine, just warm up the milk with the steam as you would for a real cappuccino. If not, I have devised a trick to get the foam going.

ingredients

300 g/11 oz mixed mushrooms (chestnut [cremini], portobello, chanterelles, pied de moutons, etc.)
1.3 litres/2¼ pints brown vegetable stock (p.159)
1 x 400 g/14 oz tin butter (lima) beans
7–8 parsley florets, roughly torn
7–8 chives, roughly torn
Salt and pepper

for the truffle oil foam

250 ml/9 fl oz /1 cup full-fat milk
½ tsp white truffle oil
2 tsp agar flakes (optional, see method)

method

Clean the mushrooms. Remove all the dirt by rubbing with a piece of slightly wet kitchen paper. Never wash mushrooms under water: they absorb it like a sponge, and it ruins their delicate taste. Cut them into 2.5 cm/1 in pieces.

Bring the stock to a boil and simmer for 5 minutes. Add the mushrooms, beans and herbs and simmer for 10 minutes. Remove the mushrooms and beans with a slotted spoon and place into a bowl. Pass the cooking stock through a fine sieve to remove any bits of dirt.

Blend the soup in two batches, mixing each batch with about 600 ml/1 pint of cooking liquid. Blend for at least 1 minute. Pour into a sieve placed on top of a soup pan. Press with the back of a spoon to extract all the liquid. Reheat gently and pour into the cappuccino cups.

If you own an espresso machine, you will know how to make frothy milk. Mix 250 ml/9 fl oz of full-fat milk with ½ teaspoon of truffle oil, and proceed as for making cappuccino foam.

If you don't own any gadgets, mix the milk, truffle oil and agar flakes and heat without stirring. Simmer for 3 minutes, stirring occasionally. Leave to cool slightly. Beat the milk with an electric hand-held mixer. Once you have removed a first batch of foam, beat again to produce more. Use quickly as the foam will not last.

Pour the soup into cappuccino cups, spoon the foam directly onto the surface, and serve at once.

Courgette & miso
with wasabi oat cream

Serves 4
Preparation: 10 minutes
Cooking time: 50 minutes

Miso is a fermented rice and soy bean preparation that comes as a paste. The choice of miso pastes in a Japanese shop is overwhelming. You should look for *shiro miso* (or white miso) which is less fermented and is sweeter but less salty than red or brown miso. Some pastes contain alcohol, but this should be written on the translated label at the back.

for the stock
150 g/5 oz fresh shiitake
mushrooms
4 strands of *wakame*
1 celery stick

for the soup
2 tbsp vegetable oil
650 g/1½ lb courgettes
(zucchini), grated
1 leek, finely chopped
Salt and pepper
3 tbsp white miso paste

for the wasabi oat cream
1½ tsp wasabi
5 tbsp dairy-free oat cream
½ tsp white miso paste

12 chives, to garnish

method

Place the shiitake mushrooms, wakame and celery in a 3-litre soup pan, cover with 1.3 litres/2¼ pints of water, bring to a boil, and simmer for 30 minutes. Remove the vegetables with a slotted spoon and discard.

Heat the oil in a large frying-pan (large enough to contain all the courgettes). Stir-fry the courgettes and leek over high heat for 3 minutes. They should become soft but should not brown. Season well with salt and freshly ground black pepper.

Add the mixture to the stock and bring to a boil. Simmer for 5 minutes and turn off the heat.

Leave to cool for 10 minutes, then whiz in 2 batches in a blender. Return the soup to the pan and reheat gently. Meanwhile, dilute 3 tablespoons of miso paste with a ladle of stock. Add the miso-stock mixture to the soup, turn off the heat, and stir well.

Meanwhile, place the wasabi in a small bowl, add a teaspoon of oat cream, and press with the back of the spoon to mix. Gradually add more cream, until well blended. Add the miso paste and mix well.

Serve the soup with drizzles of wasabi cream and decorate with long chives.

tip

Miso is always added at the last minute and should never be boiled. That would destroy its flavour.

Jabugo consommé with chicken liver dumplings

Serves 4–6
Preparation: 2 hours (stock best prepared the day before)
Cooking time: 8 minutes

We have now reached the zenith of poshness. Jabugo is the name of a town in the province of Huelva in Andalucía. It has also become a generic term for the Pata Negra ham made from this special breed of pigs, which are raised in the mountains and fed on acorns. It is the most amazing and expensive cured ham. But the trick is to get cheap Jabugo ham bones, sold in chunks and bags in Spanish shops, and to make this exceptional stock out of them.

ingredients

700 g/1 lb 9 oz Jabugo ham bones, broken into pieces
1 onion, halved
5 garlic cloves
2 bay leaves

Liver dumplings (see p.168), to serve

method

Place the ham bones, onion, garlic and bay leaves in a 4-litre soup pan. Cover with 2 litres/3½ pints of water. Bring to a boil, and remove the foamy scum that rises to the surface. Reduce the heat and simmer very gently, covered, for 1½ hours. Taste the stock. It should be full of flavour, but all bones and ham are different. Cook it for a little longer if you think it needs more flavour. Ideally, this stock should be cooked the day before and left overnight in the fridge. The following day, remove the fat at the surface and keep it: it makes a wonderful cooking fat for onions, potatoes or eggs.

Transfer the stock to a 3-litre soup pan and reheat gently.

Prepare the chicken liver dumplings. Keep in mind that the raw mixture needs to be refrigerated for 30 minutes. They are best prepared on the day. Cook them on their own for 8 minutes in simmering water, and serve with the Jabugo consommé.

Black beluga lentil soup with caper and dill sour cream

Serves 4
Preparation: 10 minutes
Cooking time: 1 hour and
15 minutes

The black lentils used here are not the Indian *urad dal* but the shiny lentils grown in North America that are also called beluga lentils. Beluga lentils are marketed as a competitor of puy lentils. However, they are very different and more mushroomy than puy lentils. Unlike other lentils, there is no need to soak them. This soup is filling – serve in small portions with a dollop of caper cream.

for the lentil soup

1.2 litres/2 pints green vegetable stock (see p.160)
2 tbsp olive oil
1 large onion, finely chopped
1 large carrot, finely chopped
175 g /6 oz black beluga lentils
2 tbsp dill

for the caper cream

1 tbsp capers in salt
300 g/11 oz sour cream
1 tbsp chives, finely chopped
1 tbsp dill, finely chopped

method

Prepare the stock as on p.160. Reserve extra liquid to thin the soup, if needed.

Heat the oil in a 3-litre soup pan, and fry the onion and carrot for 3 minutes, until just starting to brown. Add the lentils and stir-fry for a few seconds. Add the stock and bring to a boil. Boil for 5 minutes, and remove the foam that rises on the surface. Reduce the heat and simmer for 35–40 minutes. Taste the lentils: they should be soft and mushy and not '*al dente*'. Leave to cool for 15 minutes.

Meanwhile, prepare the caper cream. Soak the capers in water for 10 minutes. Drain well and chop finely. Mix the sour cream, capers, chives and dill, and season with plenty of black pepper. Place in the fridge until ready to serve.

Place half of the lentils and their cooking juices in a blender and whiz until smooth. Repeat with the other half. It should have the consistency of double cream, but you can thin it with extra vegetable stock, if needed. Return the soup to the pan, add the dill, and reheat gently, before serving.

" *This also makes a smart lunch for four, accompanied with smoked salmon and rye soda bread canapés on the side.* "

Cherry tomato soup with spiced golden butter & Parmesan crisps

Serves 4
Preparation: 10 minutes
Cooking time: 20 minutes for
the crisps + 12 minutes
for the spiced butter
+ 15 minutes for the soup

You can now find many varieties of cherry tomatoes. I have mixed them up and cooked them for a very short time to get a real taste of fresh tomatoes. This is a very simple soup, and what makes it very special is the association with the spiced butter and the Parmesan crisps.

method

In a bowl, mix the Parmesan, cornflour and freshly ground black pepper (about 6–7 turns of the peppermill) until well blended. Heat a small non-stick frying pan over a medium heat for 1 minute. Reduce the heat slightly, sprinkle some of the Parmesan mixture into a very thin layer. Leaving some small holes will create a lace effect. Cook for 2 minutes, then lift a corner with a flat spatula; the underneath should be golden. If not, your heat is not high enough. If it is burnt, the heat is obviously too high. Delicately lift the Parmesan 'crêpe' with the spatula and quickly flip over to cook the other side. Again, it should take about 1–2 minutes. Place the cooked Parmesan crisp on a baking tray and cook the next one. You can give them different shapes. Once you are an expert, you can cook 4 in a large frying pan.

for the Parmesan crisps
125 g/4 oz/generous 1 cup
Parmesan cheese, finely grated
into thin strands
1 tbsp + 1 tsp cornflour (cornstarch)
Freshly ground black pepper

To make the spiced butter, melt the butter in a small stainless steel or enamel pan. Don't use a black pan, or you won't be able to check the colour of the butter. Cook it over very low heat until it turns golden (see p.48 for more details). Immediately pour into a bowl and add the spices. Mix well and set aside to infuse.

for the spiced butter
85 g/3 oz/¾ stick butter
1 tsp ground cumin
1 tsp ground coriander
½ tsp paprika
Pinch of saffron

Heat the oil in a 3-litre soup pan. Fry the onions for 3 minutes, until they are soft and just starting to turn golden. Add the garlic and cook for 1 more minute. Add the tomatoes and sugar and cook for 5 minutes, until soft. Season well and add the spiced butter. Cook for 1 minute. Add 600 ml/1 pint of water and cook for 7 minutes. Turn off the heat and leave to cool slightly. Transfer half the mixture into a blender and process until smooth. Pass through a fine sieve to remove the skin and seeds, return to the soup pan, correct the seasoning and reheat gently.

for the cherry tomato soup
2 tbsp olive oil
2 onions, finely chopped
2 large garlic cloves, crushed
1 kg/2¼ lb cherry tomatoes
(a mixture of sweet, sun gold,
plum, on the vine), halved
2 tsp sugar

Serve the soup with the Parmesan crisps.

Cream of beans with Finnan haddock

Serves 4
Preparation: 5 minutes +
overnight to soak the beans
Cooking time: 55 minutes

Named after the fishing village of Finnan in Scotland, Finnan haddock is dried and smoked on the bone and has an exceptional flavour. You can order it through your fishmonger or on the internet.

for the cream of beans
250 g/9 oz white beans,
soaked overnight
1 small onion, peeled
1 small fennel, halved
2 garlic cloves, peeled

for the haddock
1 Finnan haddock (about 500 g/1 lb)
500 ml/18 fl oz/generous 2 cups milk
3 lime leaves
1 tsp coriander seeds
10 black peppercorns

for the soup
1 leek (150 g/5 oz)
10 g/⅓ oz/scant 1 tbsp butter
1 tsp sunflower oil
Salt and pepper

Chervil or parsley,
chopped, to garnish

tip
Buy a bag of frozen lime leaves from
a Thai shop to keep in your freezer.
Use it instead of bay leaves in fish
stocks for a special citrus touch.

method
Place the beans in a 3-litre soup pan. Cover with 1.5 litres/2¾ pints of water and bring to a boil. Boil vigorously for 10 minutes. This will help to release and eliminate the toxins contained in the beans. Skim the foam that forms at the surface. Add the onion, fennel and garlic. Gently simmer for 45 minutes. Taste the beans: they should be well cooked and almost mushy. Cook them a little longer if needed.

Place the Finnan haddock in a deep frying pan, cover with milk and add 200 ml/7 fl oz of water. Add the lime leaves, coriander and black peppercorns. Bring to a gentle simmer, then simmer for 10 minutes. Detach the flesh from the skin and bones and set aside, covered. Continue gently simmering the milk with the fish skin and bones for another 10 minutes, then pass through a sieve set on top of a bowl.

Drain the beans but keep the cooking liquid. Place half of the beans, fennel, onion and garlic with 150 ml/5 fl oz/generous ½ cup of the bean-cooking liquid, plus 150 ml/5 fl oz/generous ½ cup of the haddock-cooking liquid, in a blender and process until smooth. Pour the mixture into a sieve placed over a pan. Repeat with the other half.

Return the soup to the pan. Add more of both cooking liquids, if needed, to give it the consistency of single cream. Add the haddock flesh and reheat gently.

Meanwhile, halve the leek, cut each half into 8 cm/3 in chunks, then cut each chunk into thin strips. Heat the butter and oil in a medium frying pan. When the butter is foamy, add the leek and cook over a medium heat for 3 minutes. Season with salt and freshly ground black pepper.

Spoon the soup into bowls, pile some of the leek in the centre, and garnish with chervil or parsley. Warn your guests that some haddock bones may have escaped your eagle eye.

Prawn bisque with vanilla & star anise, garnished with pan-fried prawn in vanilla butter

Serves 4
Preparation: 15 minutes
Cooking time: 45 minutes

Vanilla, with its persistent sensuous smell, is irresistible. My favourite vanilla comes from Tahiti, but all vanillas, according to where they were grown and how they were fermented, have their special identity and character. Unfortunately, vanilla is not used enough in savoury dishes. Prawns are a perfect match. This soup is made like traditional bisque with the twist of exotic flavours.

ingredients

650 g/1 lb 7 oz whole raw king prawns (jumbo shrimp)
1 long, plump vanilla pod
30 g/1 oz/2 tbsp butter, softened
2 tbsp olive oil
2 shallots, chopped
1 carrot, chopped
½ celery stick, chopped
Salt and cayenne pepper
Small pinch of chilli powder
2 tbsp rum
100 ml/3½ fl oz/scant ½ cup dry sherry or dry white wine
1 tbsp tomato paste
40 g/1½ oz/scant ¼ cup Arborio (risotto) rice
1 tsp sugar
2 star anise
1.3 litres/2¼ pints fish stock, or water

4 tbsp double (heavy) cream, to serve

tip

The best way to keep vanilla beans is in sugar. They will perfume the sugar and keep their moisture.

method

Remove the heads and shells from 12 prawns. Keep the tails aside in the fridge: they will be cooked separately and used as a garnish. Roughly chop the rest of the prawns and mix in with the heads and shells.

Using a sharp knife, halve the vanilla pod lengthwise and scrape the seeds inside half of the pod. Mix the seeds with the butter. This flavoured butter will be used later on to pan-fry the prawns. Retain the pod.

Heat the oil in a 3-litre soup pan. Fry the shallots, carrot and celery over a medium heat for 2 minutes, until soft and bright in colour. Add the prawns, and cook until they turn bright pink. Season well with salt, a pinch of cayenne pepper, and the chilli powder. Add the rum, and let it reduce for 30 seconds. Add the dry sherry or wine, and let it reduce for 1 minute. Add the tomato paste, and stir well to dissolve it in the alcohol. Add the rice, vanilla pod, sugar, star anise, and the fish stock or water. Bring to a boil and simmer for 30 minutes.

Remove the vanilla and star anise. Place the soup in a blender and process until smooth. Pass through a fine sieve. Return the vanilla pod and star anise to the soup and reheat gently.

Meanwhile, heat the vanilla butter in a medium-sized frying pan until foamy. Add the prawn tails and cook gently for 1–2 minutes on each side.

Spoon the soup into the bowls, place 3 prawns in the centre of each, and serve. You can garnish the soup with a drop of double cream.

Moorish pumpkin soup with pumpkin seeds & saffron brioche croutons

Serves 4
Preparation: 5 minutes
Cooking time: 40 minutes

There is something very festive about pumpkin soup, maybe because it is often on the menu for special occasions. Pumpkin flesh has a lot of moisture. Baking it removes the moisture and really enhances the taste. It goes very well with the Moorish flavours of the red vegetable stock (see p.161). The croutons will quickly soak up the soup. To keep their crispiness, they are best served on the side and added as you eat the soup.

for the soup
900 g/2 lb pumpkin (giving about 650 g/1 lb 7 oz of flesh)
1 onion, peeled and cut into wedges
3 garlic cloves
1½ tbsp olive oil
Salt and pepper
About 1.2 litres/2 pints/5 cups red vegetable stock (see p.161)

for the croutons
50 g/2 oz/½ stick unsalted butter
Large pinch of saffron
125 g/4 oz one-day-old brioche bread, cubed
20 g /¾ oz/generous ⅛ cup pumpkin seeds
Salt and pepper

method

Cut the pumpkin into chunks and remove any seeds and fibres, then cut the skin off with a knife or a peeler. I find smaller chunks are easier to peel. Cover a baking tray with parchment paper and spread the pumpkin chunks, onion wedges and garlic on top. Drizzle with the olive oil and bake for 30–40 minutes. They can cook while the stock is being made.

When ready, remove the pumpkin from the oven, season with salt and freshly ground black pepper. Turn off the heat from under the stock. Leave both the pumpkin and the stock to cool for 15 minutes.

Meanwhile, melt the butter in a small saucepan. Add the saffron, turn off the heat and leave to infuse.

Squeeze the roasted garlic cloves out of their peels by pressing on each clove with the back of a spoon. Place half the pumpkin, onion and garlic in a blender, cover with 600 ml/1 pint of stock and whiz until smooth. Repeat with the other half. It should be slightly thicker than the consistency of double cream. Add some more stock if you want a thinner soup. Return the soup to the pan, adjust the seasoning, and gently reheat.

Meanwhile, heat the saffron butter in a medium-sized frying pan. Add the brioche cubes and pumpkin seeds. Cook for 2–3 minutes, turning the cubes and stirring the seeds so that they are golden on all sides. Season lightly with salt and pepper.

Serve the soup garnished with a few cubes and seeds. Place the remaining cubes and seeds in little dishes on the side of each plate.

Asparagus & coconut soup with steamed coriander meringue

Serves 4
Preparation: 15 minutes
Cooking time: 30 minutes

for the soup
800 g/1¾ lb asparagus
1 tbsp vegetable oil
15 g/½ oz galangal, peeled and sliced
2 lemongrass stalks, finely sliced
30 g/1 oz shallots, finely chopped
2 tsp sugar
1 x 400 ml/14 fl oz tin reduced-fat coconut milk
3 frozen lime leaves
1 Thai red chilli, sliced in half
150 ml/5 fl oz/⅔ cup coconut cream

for the meringue
2 egg whites
1 tsp lime juice
Salt and pepper
2 tbsp fresh coriander (cilantro), finely chopped

This soup is designed especially for vegetarians. The galangal must be stir-fried until really golden brown, as this is crucial for the flavour. The savoury meringue is beaten at the last minute, then poached in the soup. It makes an airy garnish that goes really well with coconut. I use reduced-fat coconut because I prefer its lightness in soup, and I add coconut cream to enrich it at the last minute.

method
Cut the asparagus tips and reserve. Chop the rest of the asparagus, place in a 3-litre soup pan, cover with 800 ml/1½ pints of water, bring to a boil and simmer for 10 minutes. Turn off the heat and leave to cool for 15 minutes.

Place half of the asparagus and liquid into a blender and whiz until smooth. Pour into a sieve set over a bowl. Repeat with the other half. Stir the asparagus purée to extract as much juice as possible and set aside.

Rinse the pan used to cook the asparagus. Heat the oil in it and fry the galangal, lemongrass, shallots and sugar over a medium heat for 3 minutes. They should be well browned and crispy. Add the asparagus stock, coconut milk, lime leaves and chilli. Bring to a gentle boil, stirring all the time so that the coconut milk doesn't curdle. Simmer for 10 minutes.

Meanwhile, place the egg whites in a medium-sized bowl, add the lime juice and a pinch of salt. Whiz with an electric handmixer, until the egg is fluffy and hard peaks form. Add the coriander and mix for just 2 seconds.

Bring 1 litre/1¾ pints of water to simmering point in a large frying pan. With two large spoons, form quenelles out of the beaten egg and drop into the simmering water. Cook for 1½ minutes, delicately turn over, and cook for 1½ minutes more. Remove and place directly in serving bowls.

Add the asparagus tips and coconut cream to the soup, and simmer for 5 minutes. Ladle the soup and asparagus tips into the bowls with the steamed meringue, and serve.

Celeriac with sorrel herb cream

Serves 4
Preparation: 10 minutes
Cooking time: 50 minutes

Sorrel is a wild herb that grows everywhere in France. It is very acidic when cooked and is often mixed with spinach to temper the taste. It is a bit of a shock for me to buy five leaves of sorrel packaged in a sealed plastic bag when I would normally buy it by the handful for nearly nothing. So I have respected the packaging and used it sparingly to flavour the cream for this celeriac soup.

for the celeriac soup
750 g/1 lb 11 oz celeriac
1 small leek
1 medium carrot
Small handful of flat-leaf parsley
2½ tbsp olive oil
1 tbsp yellow mustard seeds
1 onion, roughly chopped
35 g/1¼ oz shallots, roughly chopped

for the sorrel herb cream
200 ml/7 fl oz/generous ¾ cup single (light) cream
5 tbsp sorrel, finely chopped
2 tbsp chives, finely chopped
2 tbsp chervil, finely chopped
Salt and pepper

Extra chervil, for garnish

method
Wash the celeriac and peel. Place the peels in a 3-litre soup pan. Cut the celeriac in 2.5 cm/1 in cubes and set aside. Cut the leek and carrot into big chunks and add to the pan. Add the parsley, cover with 1.5 litres/2¾ pints of water and bring to a boil. Reduce the heat and simmer for 30 minutes. When ready, pass the stock through a fine sieve and reserve.

Heat the oil over a medium heat in a 3-litre soup pan, add the mustard seeds, and cook for 1 minute until they start to pop. Add the onion, shallots and celeriac chunks, and stir-fry for 2 minutes. Reduce the heat and cook for 5 minutes, stirring occasionally, until the celeriac starts to soften slightly and become golden. Add about 1 litre/1¾ pints of stock and cook for 15–20 minutes, until tender.

Place one-third of the celeriac and stock in a blender and whiz until smooth. Repeat with the rest of the celeriac. Add some of the vegetable stock, if needed. The soup should be slightly thicker than single cream. Return to the soup pan, adjust the seasoning, and reheat gently.

Meanwhile, place the single cream and herbs in a small saucepan. Heat gently but do not let it boil. Season, and leave to infuse for 5 minutes.

Serve the soup garnished with chervil leaves and a little shot glass of the sorrel cream on the side. Pour some of the cream in the soup and add more as you are eating it.

Velouté of fennel & fish with a hint of Pastis

Serves 4–6
Preparation: 15 minutes
+ 40 minutes to make
the fish stock
Cooking time: 30 minutes

Velouté is a sensuous word that means 'velvety'. It perfectly describes the consistency of this soup. Pastis is an anise-based aperitif originally from Marseilles, which was invented in the 1920s to replace the banned Absinthe. A dash of Pastis stirred into the soup just before serving will enhance the fennel and make you feel like you're on holiday.

ingredients
800 ml/1½ pints fish stock
800 g/1¾ lb fennel
3 tbsp olive oil
1 onion, chopped
2–3 tbsp Pernod Pastis

method
Follow the recipe for fish stock on p.162.

Trim the leaves on top of the fennel and reserve for garnish. Halve the fennel, remove the hard core and thinly slice.

Heat the oil in a 3-litre soup pan. Add the onion, and cook over a medium heat for 5 minutes, until soft and slightly caramelized on the edges. Add the fennel, stir-fry for a few minutes, then cook, covered, for 15 minutes. It should be soft but not brown. Fennels are starchy and will stick to the bottom of the pan, so stir from time to time to make sure nothing burns. Add the fish stock, bring to a simmer, and cook for another 15 minutes.

Turn off the heat and leave to cool for 15–20 minutes. Blend in batches. Fennel can be fibrous; pass through a fine sieve set over a pan, if needed.

Reheat the soup gently. Add the Pernod, according to your taste, and serve garnished with fennel tops.

❝ Serve this soup garnished with oysters for an extra special treat. ❞

Cream of sweetcorn with Tequila-marinated avocado & puffed corn

Serves 4–6
Preparation: 15 minutes
Cooking time: 25 minutes

Popcorn makes a really interesting and unique soup garnish. In this soup, I have used fresh sweetcorn rather than frozen in order to use the cobs as a base for the stock. Tarragon is perfect with sweetcorn, and the cubes of avocado, marinated in lime and Tequila, add a real punch.

ingredients

1.5 kg/3 lb 5 oz fresh sweetcorn (corn)
½ lime
3 tbsp olive oil
1 large onion, peeled and finely chopped
1 tbsp olive oil
40 g/1½ oz/⅓ cup popcorn maize
2–3 tbsp tarragon, chopped
75 ml/3 fl oz/⅓ cup single (light) cream
2 small avocados
Zest of 1 lime
Juice of 2 limes
2 to 3 tbsp Tequila
Salt and pepper

66 For the best effect, serve this soup in glass teacups or small heatproof glasses. 99

method

Cut the corn kernels off the stem by standing them upright in a bowl and sliding a large knife down its length. You should obtain about 500–600 g/1 lb–1 lb 5 oz of corn kernels. Place the corn stems in a non-metallic 3-litre soup pan (they tend to oxidize) with half a lime squeezed and dropped into the pan. Cover with 1.5 litres/2¾ pints of water and bring to a boil. Simmer, uncovered, for 20 minutes.

Meanwhile, heat the oil in a large frying pan, and fry the onion over a medium heat for 3 minutes, until soft and just starting to brown. Add the corn kernels to the frying pan and stir-fry over high heat for 6–7 minutes, until the corn starts to caramelize and has a lovely golden colour. The starch from the kernels will stick to the bottom of the pan and burn, but don't worry, this is part of the taste; just stir and scrape constantly. Remove from the heat and tip into a 3-litre soup pan.

Heat the oil in a pan fitted with a lid. Add the popcorn maize and cook over a medium heat for 3–4 minutes, shaking the pan from time to time, until all the corn has popped. Do not open the lid, or the corn will pop out. Season and set aside for garnish.

By this time, the stock will be almost ready. Strain it and add 1.2 litres/2 pints to the onion and kernels. Bring to a simmer and cook for 10 minutes. Add the chopped tarragon and simmer for 2 more minutes.

Blend the soup in two batches and pass through a very fine sieve set over a pan to eliminate all the corn skins. Adjust the seasoning (add more tarragon if needed), add the cream, and reheat gently for a few minutes. Do not let it boil.

While the soup is reheating, dice the avocados, and season with the zest, lime juice and Tequila. Serve the soup, topped with some popcorn, avocado dices and tarragon. Place the rest of the popcorn and avocado on the table.

all in one

Soups lend themselves to be more than starters. Chunky soups make fabulous main courses. I love the concept of surrounding a dish with different accompaniments, and I have applied it to most of the soups in this section. Goulash will be more filling with potato dumplings, or *knödel*. Marinated onions will add crunchiness to a black bean soup. Chickpea pancakes can be dunked like bread. All these preparations will add texture, taste and fun.

The recipes in this section are designed for six. They are not more complicated than any of the other soups. They are just a bit more involved because, in addition to the soup, you will need to prepare the garnishes. If you fancy some of the soups in smaller quantities, you will notice that some recipes can easily be halved and turned into a starter for four.

And if you are wondering how to organize a meal around these main-course soups, they call for casual tapas with a drink as a starter and any of your favourite desserts as a follow-up.

Goulash with potato *knödel* & sour cream

Serves 6 (half the recipe
will make a starter for 4)
Preparation: 25 minutes
Cooking time: 40 minutes
+ 2½ hours simmering

Goulash is a well-known Hungarian dish that can be prepared both as a stew and a soup. It is traditionally cooked with potatoes, but I prefer to garnish it with potato dumplings, or *knödel*, instead (see p.169). Beef cheek is extremely tender and tasty, and perfect for braising. You might have to order it from your butcher.

ingredients
6 tbsp cooking olive oil
1.5 kg/3 lb 5 oz beef cheek,
cut into 2 cm/¾ in pieces
4 onions, peeled and finely sliced
150 g/5 oz red (bell) peppers,
deseeded and finely sliced
50 g/2 oz small green (bell) peppers,
deseeded and finely sliced
3 garlic cloves, crushed
1½ tsp caraway seeds
1½ tbsp Hungarian paprika
2 tsp fresh oregano, chopped
2 x 400 g/14 oz good-quality tinned
Italian chopped tomatoes
½ tsp sugar
Salt and pepper
2 litres/3½ pints beef stock
(see p.157)

Potato knödel (see p.169)
and sour cream to serve

method
Heat 2 tablespoons of the oil in a large frying pan until very hot. Add half of the beef and fry until well browned, stirring occasionally. Season and place the cooked meat in a 4-litre soup pan, set over a low heat. Repeat with the other half of the meat. Make sure that the meat is at room temperature. Cold meat will drop the temperature of the pan and will not brown as well.

After all the beef has been cooked, add the rest of the oil, reduce the heat to medium, and fry the onions for 6–7 minutes. (They will quickly brown because of the meat juices in the pan. This is fine, but make sure that they don't burn.) Add the onions to the soup pan.

Now fry the peppers for 6–7 minutes. They should be soft and slightly brown on the edges. Season halfway through. Add them to the soup pan.

With a pestle and mortar, crush the garlic, caraway seeds, oregano and paprika to a paste. Add the mixture to the frying pan and fry for 30 seconds. Add the tinned tomatoes and sugar and season with salt and pepper. Bring to a boil and let it bubble away for 10 minutes. Add the spiced tomatoes to the soup pan, pour 1.5 litres/2¾ pints of beef stock on top, and simmer gently, partly covered, for 2 hours.

After 2 hours of cooking, the liquid may have reduced too much. Add more stock, if needed, and let it simmer for another 30 minutes.

Just before serving, heat a large saucepan of water until simmering and cook the *knödel* for 5 minutes. Remove with a slotted spoon and place in a warm dish with a knob of butter. Your guests can help themselves to *knödel* and sour cream.

Vietnamese hot pot

Serves 6
Preparation: 35 minutes
(+ 1 hour to part-freeze
the sirloin)
Cooking time: 35 minutes

A hot pot makes for fun and stress-free entertaining. You don't have to worry about your cooking skills because the guests do the cooking. You will need some specialized equipment that can be found in Oriental shops: a portable gas stove to simmer the stock on the table, small wire baskets to cook the food and chopsticks.

method

Place all the dipping sauce ingredients into a bowl and mix well. Leave in the fridge for at least 1 hour. You can prepare it the day before, as it will taste even better. This sauce is made with fresh ingredients and will keep for only 2–3 days.

Place the tamarind in a small saucepan, cover with 300 ml/½ pint of water and simmer for 10 minutes. Strain and set the tamarind stock aside.

Heat the oil in a 3-litre saucepan and fry the lemongrass, shallots, garlic and ginger until golden. Add the tamarind stock, 2 litres/3½ pints of water, the stock cubes and sugar. Simmer for 20 minutes. (You can also use homemade chicken stock, but I think chicken stock cubes work well in this case.)

Meanwhile prepare the other ingredients:
Cut the sirloin into very thin slices. For paper thin slices, place the sirloin in the freezer for 1 hour before slicing. Arrange the beef slices and beansprouts on one plate, all the seafood on another, and the shredded vegetables on a third one.

Place the rice vermicelli in a bowl, cover with boiling water and leave for 5 minutes. Drain and rinse under cold water. Arrange the vermicelli on a platter with the mint and coriander.

Add the sliced spring onions to the soup stock and place over a portable gas heater in the centre of the table. Place all the other ingredients on the table. Divide the dipping sauce between three small bowls. Now the fun can start! Each guest places some of the ingredients in their wire basket and plunges it into the simmering stock to cook for about 1 minute. They tip the contents of the basket into a bowl and add herbs, dipping sauce, noodles and stock, according to their taste. As the evening goes by, the stock becomes richer and even more delicious.

tip

Make sure your portable gas fire and stock pot are very stable. Use a wide stock pot rather than a tall one. It's easier to cook all the baskets at once.

for the sauce

150 ml/5 fl oz/⅔ cup *mâm nêm*
(Vietnamese anchovy sauce),
or fish sauce
100 g/3½ oz pineapple,
finely chopped
2 large garlic cloves,
finely chopped
1–2 Thai red chillies, finely sliced
Juice of 1 lime
4 tbsp sugar

for the stock

150 g/5 oz tamarind, with seeds
1 tbsp groundnut oil
2 lemongrass stalks,
finely chopped
100 g/3½ oz/⅔ cup shallots,
finely chopped
3 garlic cloves, crushed
25 g/1oz ginger, finely chopped
2 organic chicken stock cubes
2 tbsp sugar
5 spring onions (scallions),
finely sliced

for the soup

500 g/1 lb 2 oz beef sirloin
500 g/1 lb 2 oz beansprouts
300 g/11 oz raw prawns (shrimp)
300 g/11 oz squid rings
6 scallops
1 large Chinese leaf
2 carrots, shredded
250 g/9 oz/2½ cups mangetout
(snow peas)
250 g/9 oz rice vermicelli
1 bunch each of fresh mint
and coriander (cilantro)

Bean and duck confit with *cavolo nero*

Serves 6 (half the recipe will
make a starter for 4)
Preparation: 15 minutes,
+ 6 hours for confit,
+ 7 hours for beans
Cooking time: 1 hour

Confit is a great way to preserve duck or goose. The duck parts are first cured in salt, then slowly cooked in fat. Duck confit is a versatile dish that can be slowly reheated under the grill and served with garlic potatoes and a salad, or added to soups. Don't be put off by the many steps in this recipe. The duck confit, stock and beans can be prepared in advance. You can also buy jars of duck or goose confit in speciality shops.

for the duck confit

4 duck legs
125 g/4 oz coarse sea salt
350 g/12 oz duck fat
5 cloves garlic
2 bay leaves
12 peppercorns

for the beans

200 g/7 oz small white beans,
soaked for at least 6 hours in water
1 large fennel
3 garlic cloves
2 cloves
20 peppercorns

for the soup

3 tbsp duck fat from the confit
3 onions, peeled and sliced
1 large carrot
300 g/11 oz turnips
175 g/6 oz leeks
1.5 litres/2¾ pints chicken stock

for the garnishes

2 tbsp duck fat from the confit
2 large cloves garlic
160 g/5½ oz dried mixed white and
brown breadcrumbs (see p.172)
250 g/9 oz *cavolo nero*

method

The day before, make the duck confit. Place the duck legs in a non-reactive dish, and press the salt over both sides of the legs. Leave in the fridge for 4 hours. Remove from the fridge, wash off the salt and drain well on kitchen roll. Place in a heavy 3-litre pan. Add the duck fat and slowly bring to a simmer; the fat will melt and cover the duck legs. Add the garlic, bay leaves and peppercorns, and barely simmer (use a heat diffuser), partly covered, for 2 hours. Leave to cool. When cool, shred the meat off the bone and keep it in duck fat until ready to use. Keep the bones for your stock pot. Reserve the remainder of the fat for cooking.

Drain the beans. Place in a 4-litre pan, cover with 2.5 litres/4½ pints of water, and bring to a boil. Boil vigorously for 10 minutes. Remove the foam that forms at the surface. Add the fennel, garlic, cloves and peppercorn, and simmer for 1 hour.

When the beans are ready, drain and set aside. Use the same pot to make the soup. Heat 3 tablespoons of duck fat over medium heat. Add onions and cook for 12 minutes, until well caramelized. Add the rest of the vegetables, and cook for 5 more minutes, seasoning with salt halfway through. Add the beans and stock, bring to a simmer, and cook for 30 minutes.

Slowly reheat the duck meat in a large frying pan to melt the fat. Take out the duck meat and add to the soup. Bring the soup back to a simmer and cook for 7–8 minutes. Skim off the foam and fat that forms at the surface.

Heat the fat left in the frying pan over medium heat. Add the garlic, and cook for 30 seconds. Add the breadcrumbs and pan-fry for 2–3 minutes, until crisp and golden. Transfer to a serving bowl and set aside. Add a little more fat to the pan, add the *cavolo nero*, and stir-fry for 2 minutes. Add about 100 ml/3½ fl oz/ scant ½ cup of water, cover, and cook for 3 minutes. Transfer to a serving bowl. Serve the soup with the *cavolo nero* and breadcrumbs on the side.

Chunky tomato soup with baked polenta dumplings

Serves 6
(with 18–20 dumplings)
Preparation: 40 minutes
+ 1 hour to cool the peppers
Cooking time: 50 minutes

for the marinated peppers
6 long Romano peppers
1 large garlic clove, finely sliced
Salt and pepper
1 tsp balsamic vinegar
2 tbsp extra-virgin olive oil

for the soup
1.3 kg/3 lb tomatoes
2 tbsp olive oil
2 large onions, chopped
4 garlic cloves, crushed
1/2 tsp sugar
Salt and pepper
1.8 litres/4 pints red vegetable stock
(see p.161)

for the baked polenta dumplings
500 ml/18 fl oz/generous 2 cups milk
125 g/41/2 oz/3/4 cup instant polenta
1/2 tsp freshly grated nutmeg
Salt and pepper
2 eggs
50 g/13/4 oz/1/2 cup grated Parmesan

Flat-leaf parsley or basil, to garnish

These baked polenta dumplings are a family recipe. They were covered with Parmesan and baked in tomato sauce, sometimes served with a fried egg on top. As a kid, I thought there couldn't be a better dish in the world. These polenta dumplings are also wonderful in soups. You could poach them, but I love the added crustiness of baking them.

method

Preheat the grill to maximum. Place the peppers on a baking tray lined with foil and grill for 20 minutes, turning the peppers halfway through. They should be well blackened. Place in a bowl and cover with clingfilm until cool enough to handle. The steam trapped in the bowl will help the skins to detach.

When cool enough to handle, remove the skins and seeds, and cut the peppers into strips. Place the strips in a bowl with the garlic. Season well and add the balsamic vinegar. Toss to dissolve the salt, add the oil, and mix well. Leave aside at room temperature.

Prepare the polenta dumplings. Heat the milk in a medium saucepan. Sprinkle the polenta over the top. Stir well until it thickens. Remove from the heat, season with salt, freshly ground black pepper and grated nutmeg, and leave to cool.

Peel (see p.142) and roughly chop the tomatoes. Heat the oil in a 4-litre soup pan. Add the onion and cook over a medium heat for 6–7 minutes, until soft and slightly caramelized. Add the garlic, and cook for 1 minute, until golden but not brown. Watch it carefully, as it will go from golden to brown in a few seconds. Add the tomatoes, and bring to a boil. Add the sugar and seasoning, and cook for 5 minutes, until the tomatoes are starting to lose their shape but before they turn to mush. Add the stock, bring to a boil and simmer for 20 minutes.

Preheat the oven to 180°C/350°F/Gas Mark 4. Add the eggs to the polenta mixture, one at a time, and stir well after adding each egg. Correct the seasoning if necessary. With wet hands, form 18 balls and flatten each slightly. Place on a baking tray lined with baking paper. Sprinkle some grated Parmesan over each dumpling, and bake for 15 minutes.

Serve the soup with warm dumplings and marinated peppers. Garnish with fresh flat-leaf parsley or basil leaves.

Mexican chicken soup

Serves 6
Preparation: 10 minutes
Cooking time: 2 hours

Every country has a recipe for chicken soup. I really like Jewish chicken soup served with matzo balls. You will find the recipe for matzo balls in the dumpling section (see p.166). Because it is not as well known, I have included here the recipe for '*caldo de pollo*', a Mexican chicken soup that is normally served with a myriad of garnishes and a squeeze of lime for the final kick.

ingredients

500 g/1 lb 2 oz chicken wings
1 small chicken
2 onions, diced
6 garlic cloves, peeled
1 leek, finely sliced
2 large carrots, diced
2 celery sticks, diced
2 sprigs thyme
2 bay leaves
2 dried long chillies

for the garnishes

6 limes, cut into quarters
½ lettuce, shredded
3 tomatoes, finely chopped
3 Serrano chillies, finely chopped
200 g/7 oz crumbly cheese (such as Lancashire)
6 spring onions (scallions), finely chopped
1 bunch of coriander (cilantro), chopped
2 large avocados

18 corn or flour tortillas

method

Preheat the oven to 220°C/425°F/Gas Mark 7. Place the chicken wings on a baking tray and bake for 45 minutes.

Meanwhile, place the chicken in a 4-litre soup pan. Cover with 3 litres/5 pints of boiling water from the kettle and bring to a boil. Skim the foam and fat that rises to the surface. Add the vegetables, bring back to a simmer, and cook, partly covered, for 45 minutes. Add the roasted chicken wings. Add 200 ml/7 fl oz/generous ¾ cup of water to the roasting tray, scrape the bottom to remove the bits, and add to the stock. Cook for 45 more minutes. Skim the surface from time to time.

About 20 minutes before the end of the cooking time, prepare the garnishes — except for the avocados and tortillas, which will be done at the last minute. Put everything in individual bowls and cover with clingfilm. Do not place in the fridge as they would then be too cold for the soup.

Remove the chicken and wings from the stock and leave to cool slightly. Shred all the meat off the bones. Return the shredded meat to the soup. The meat on the wings will have lost all its taste, but you can use the carcass and the chicken wings again to make another stock (which will be lighter in taste).

Preheat the oven to 160°C/325°F/Gas Mark 3.

Dice the avocados (see method on p.18). Squeeze one of the limes on top to prevent discoloration. Place in a bowl on the table, with the other ingredients.

Wrap the tortillas in baking paper and wrap again in foil. Seal the package well and place in the oven for 10 minutes. Serve the tortillas warm, wrapped in a towel.

Serve the soup piping hot in warm bowls. The garnishes will slightly cool the soup to make it the perfect temperature for eating. Add the garnishes to the soup, squeeze some lime into it, and eat with the warm tortillas.

Soupe à l'oignon gratinée

Serves 6 (half the recipe
will make a starter for 4)
Preparation: 25 minutes
Cooking time: 1 hour 20 minutes

Being Parisian, I couldn't decently write a soup book without including the famous onion soup. The soup is originally from Lyons, but it has become the standard snack for all-night party-goers. The *Pied De Cochon* is a restaurant in Les Halles in Paris which stays open 24 hours. The tradition is to gather there in the early hours to devour this comforting soup, which is the most delicious cure for hangovers. Serve at the end of a really good party!

ingredients

900 g/2 lb onions
100 g/3½ oz shallots
60 g/2½ oz/generous ½ stick butter
1 tbsp olive oil
Salt and pepper
2 tbsp plain (all-purpose) flour
200 ml/7 fl oz/generous ¾ cup white wine
2.25 litres/3½ pints/8 cups chicken stock, or water
1 large baguette
2 large garlic cloves
250 g/9 oz mixed Gruyère and Emmenthal cheese, grated

method

Peel and finely slice the onions and shallots. Try to cut slices of similar sizes so that the onions and shallots will cook and brown evenly.

Heat the butter and oil in a heavy 4-litre soup pan. The oil is mixed with the butter to prevent it from burning too fast when melted over high heat. It is good to use a heavy pan for this recipe because the onions are going to cook for a long time and you don't want them to burn at the bottom.

Add the sliced onions and shallots and cook over medium heat for 5 minutes, until the onions are soft. Reduce the heat, and cook for about 40 minutes, checking the pan regularly and stirring. After 15–20 minutes of cooking time, the onions will start to colour. You really want to get them caramelized, darker than the colour of an onion peel. This will make all the difference to the taste.

When you have obtained the right colour, season and sprinkle the flour over the onions. Cook for 1 minute, stirring all the time. Add the wine, and cook for 2 minutes more. You might have to raise the heat at this point. Add the stock or water, skim the surface, and cook for 20 minutes.

Meanwhile, preheat the grill to maximum. Cut the baguette into 2 cm/¾ in slices. Lay the slices on a baking tray and place under the grill until well toasted. Turn and toast the other side. With the tip of a fork, prick the garlic cloves and rub the toasted slices with them.

Pour the soup into ovenproof bowls, place slices of bread on top, cover with grated cheese, and place under the grill for 4–7 minutes, until the cheese is bubbly and golden.

" This recipe will make 10–12 small portions to serve at the end of a party. "

Indian bouillabaisse with saffron aïoli and fried potatoes

Serves 6
Preparation: 45 minutes
Cooking time: 55 minutes

ingredients
900 g/2 lb fish fillets
6 scallops
Salt and pepper
Juice of 1 large lime
1 kg/2¼ lb tomatoes
6 large garlic cloves
2 tsp coarsely grated ginger
3 tbsp groundnut (peanut) oil
2 tsp mustard seeds
600 g/1 lb 5 oz onions, finely sliced
25 fresh curry leaves
1 tbsp ground coriander
2 tsp ground cumin
1 tsp turmeric
¼–½ tsp chilli powder
1.3 litres/2 pints/5 cups fish stock
(see p.162)
500 g/1 lb 2 oz mussels, soaked for
1 hour, then scrubbed and bearded

for the fried potatoes
150 ml/5 fl oz/²⁄₃ cup groundnut
(peanut) oil
500 g/1 lb 2 oz baking potatoes,
peeled and diced
Salt
Pinch of cumin
Pinch of chilli powder

Saffron aïoli (p.184) and naan bread,
to serve

I had the great opportunity to make bouillabaisse with a charismatic chef from the south of France: Guy Gedda. The fish he used for the stock were fluorescent green, orange and blue. These 'poissons de roche' (fish that live in the rocks) were a feast for the eyes. After tasting that amazing stock, I realised that the identity of a bouillabaisse is directly linked to these colourful little fish and cannot be reproduced anywhere else in the world. So, I have played with Indian flavours to produce a fusion bouillabaisse with which I am really happy. Avoid oily fish, which might overpower the taste of the soup.

method
Cut the fish into 2.5 cm/1 in chunks and lay on a tray with the scallops. Season and drizzle with the lime juice. Cover with clingfilm and set aside at room temperature.

Preheat the oven to 180°C/350°F/Gas Mark 4. With a sharp knife, score a light cross on the bottom of each tomato. Place them in a bowl and cover with boiling water. Wait 1 minute. Drain, refresh under cold water, and peel. Quarter the tomatoes and place in a baking dish. Scatter the garlic and ginger over, season well with salt and drizzle with 1 tablespoon of oil. Place in the oven and bake for 35 minutes. The tomatoes should be soft but still holding their shape.

Heat the remaining oil in a frying pan, and add the mustard seeds. When they start to pop, add the onions. Stir-fry for 2 minutes over medium heat until they start to soften. Reduce the heat slightly, and cook on for 10 minutes. They should be a dark caramel colour, without being burnt. Add the curry leaves and cook for 2 more minutes, stirring all the time. Add the spices and cook for 1 minute, until the mixture starts to dry out and stick to the bottom. Add 200 ml/7 fl oz/ generous ¾ cup of fish stock, and stir well to scrape the bottom. Transfer the liquid to a 4-litre soup pan, add the rest of the fish stock and bring to a simmer.

Take the tomatoes out of the oven. Press on the garlic cloves to extract the pulp and add this with the tomatoes to the soup pan. Simmer gently for 15 minutes. Meanwhile, heat the oil in a large frying pan and cook the diced potatoes for 7–8 minutes until well golden, stirring from time to time. Drain on kitchen roll and season well with salt, a large pinch of cumin and a pinch of chilli.

Add the fish, scallops and mussels to the pan and simmer for 3 minutes. Add the fried potatoes, turn off the heat, and leave to sit for 5 minutes while you warm up the naans in the oven. Then serve with saffron aïoli and the naan bread.

Borscht with cabbage *pirojkis*

Serves 6
Preparation: 45 minutes
(make stock and dough the
day before if possible)
Cooking time: 1 hour

ingredients

1.8 litres/3¼ pints beef stock (see p.157)
2 tbsp vegetable oil
2 onions, peeled and cubed
250 g/9 oz cooked beetroot(beet),
peeled and cubed
300 g/11 oz carrots, peeled and cubed
300 g/11 oz swede, peeled and cubed
300 g/11 oz baking potatoes,
peeled and cubed
2 celery sticks, cubed
Salt and pepper
3 garlic cloves, crushed
1 tbsp tomato paste
200 g/7 oz cabbage, finely sliced
1 tbsp salt
250 g/9 oz cooked beetroot (beet) in
vinegar, grated

for the cabbage *pirojkis*

1 recipe for *pirojki* dough (p.179)
300 g/11 oz cabbage, finely sliced
1 tbsp salt
30 g/1 oz/¼ stick butter
1 tbsp vegetable oil
1 onion, finely sliced
2 large eggs, hard boiled and chopped
3 tbsp dill, chopped
Salt and pepper
1 egg, lightly beaten

Sour cream and dill, to serve

Borscht is Ukraine's national dish. It is an art to make and it starts with top-quality beef stock. Beetroot marinated in vinegar is added at the end to give the soup its slight sour aftertaste. Borscht is traditionally served with *pirojki*, a soft, brioche-like pastry, filled with creamy cabbage and dill. You can make a vegetarian version of this soup using a rich mushroom stock (see p.159) instead of beef stock.

method

Make the beef stock the day before. Remove the fat from the surface before using.

First, make the *pirojkis*. (If you have prepared the dough in advance, take it out of the fridge.) Sprinkle the cabbage with the salt and cover with boiling water. Leave for 10 minutes. Drain, rinse and set aside. Heat the butter and oil in a frying pan. Add the onion and cook over medium heat for 2–3 minutes. Add the cabbage, cover and cook for 10–15 minutes, until soft. Remove from the heat, add the chopped eggs and dill. Season and stir until well blended. Leave to cool.

Divide the dough into 18 balls. Using a rolling pin, flatten each one into a 10 cm/ 4 in disc. Place about 1½ tablespoons of the cabbage filling in the centre and draw the edges together to close. Seal by pinching the dough along the top. Turn the *pirojkis* (keeping the seam underneath) and place on a baking tray lined with baking paper. They should have a plump centre with pointy ends. Leave to rise for 20 minutes while you preheat the oven to 220°C/425°F/Gas Mark 7.

Heat the oil in a 4 litre soup pan. Add the chopped vegetables and cook for 7–8 minutes over a medium heat until slightly caramelized. Season halfway through. Add the garlic and tomato paste and cook for another minute. Add the beef stock, bring to a boil, reduce the heat and simmer for 25 minutes.

Place the sliced cabbage for the soup in a bowl. Add the salt and cover with boiling water. Leave for 10 minutes. Drain, rinse and set aside. When the soup is ready, add the cabbage to the soup and cook for 15 minutes.

Meanwhile, brush the *pirojkis* with the beaten egg, and bake for 12–15 minutes, until puffed and golden. Take out of the oven.

Add the grated beetroot to the soup, turn off the heat, cover and leave for 10 minutes. Serve the soup with the *pirojkis*, sour cream and the extra dill.

Moroccan-style vegetables with onion compote & pancakes

Serves 6
Preparation: 20 minutes +
making the stock
Cooking time: 1 hour

This soup is extremely Moorish and will raise the question: 'You're sure you didn't use meat stock in this?' It is a little involved, but all the garnishes really turn this soup into a special treat. You can make the whole dish the day before and just cook the pancakes at the last minute.

for the soup

2.3 litres/3¾ pints red vegetable stock (see p.161)
4 tbsp olive oil
2 large onions
300 g/11 oz carrots
200 g/7 oz swede
300 g/11 oz courgettes (zucchini)
200 g/7 oz aubergines (eggplants)
300 g/11 oz butternut squash
Salt and pepper

for the onion and sultana compote

2 tbsp olive oil
85 g/3 oz/½ cup sultanas (golden raisins)
4 onions, chopped
1 tsp sugar
Pinch of chilli powder

for 12 small or 6 large pancakes

175 g/6 oz/1¼ cups gram (besan) flour
175 g/6 oz/1¼ cups plain (all-purpose) flour
2¼ tsp baking powder
2¼ tsp ground cumin
¾ tsp salt
Pinch of chilli powder
1 medium egg
400 ml/14 fl oz/1¾ cups water
50 g/2 oz/½ stick butter, melted

Harissa, to serve (p.185)

method

Peel and chop all the soup vegetables in 1.5 cm/½ in pieces. Heat 2 tablespoons of olive oil in a 4-litre soup pan. Add the onions, carrots and swede. Cook over medium heat for 7–8 minutes, stirring occasionally until the vegetables are soft and slightly caramelized. Season halfway through. Add the stock, bring to a boil, then reduce the heat and simmer, partly covered, for 25 minutes.

Heat 2 tablespoons of olive oil in a large frying pan. Add the courgettes, aubergine and squash. Cook over medium heat for 10 minutes. Season and set aside.

Now start the compote. Place the sultanas in a bowl and cover with 4 tablespoons of soup stock. Heat the oil in a medium frying pan, add the onions, and cook over high heat for 2 minutes. Reduce the heat, cover, and cook gently for 10 minutes. Place the frying pan over a heat diffuser if needed.

By now, the soup will have cooked for 25 minutes. Add the stir-fried vegetables to the soup, partly cover, and simmer for another 20 minutes.

Add 1 teaspoon of sugar to the onion compote, season with salt, add a pinch of chilli powder, and cook, covered, for another 10 minutes. Check from time to time that the onions are not burning. They should gradually reduce and caramelize. Continue cooking until the pancakes are ready.

To prepare the pancakes, sieve the flours, baking powder, cumin, salt and chilli into a bowl. Gradually mix in the water until well blended, but do not overmix the batter. Heat a large frying pan and brush with melted butter. Pour three circles of batter into the pan and cook for 1 minute, until bubbles form on the surface. Flip and cook on the other side for 1 minute. Repeat with the rest of the batter. Slide onto a plate and keep warm in a 110°C/225°F/Gas Mark ¼ oven.

Serve the soup with the pancakes, the onion compote and harissa on the side.

Black bean soup & marinated red onions

Serves 6 (half the recipe
will make a starter for 4)
Preparation: 30 minutes
+ overnight soaking of the beans
Cooking time: 2½ hours

Black beans are also called 'black turtle beans' because of their hard, dark shells. They are different from red kidney beans; they have a deeper, richer flavour and are amazing in soups. Here, they are cooked 'rancho'-style and served with corn bread and marinated onions. This soup is vegetarian, but it is also delicious served with slow-roasted pork belly and crackling.

ingredients

250 g/9 oz black beans
1 large onion, finely chopped
2 bay leaves
900 g/2 lb tomatoes
400 g/14 oz courgettes (zucchini)
150 g/5 oz red (bell) peppers, deseeded
150 g/5 oz green (bell) peppers, deseeded
8 large garlic cloves
2 tbsp fresh oregano, chopped
1 heaped tbsp ground cumin
1 pinch chilli powder
3 tbsp vegetable oil
3 tbsp chipotle paste, or
3 tinned chipotles

for the marinated red onions

2 small red onions, peeled and thinly sliced
Pinch of salt
1 orange
1 small jalapeño chilli, sliced
150 ml/5 fl oz/⅔ cup cider vinegar
75 ml/3 fl oz/⅓ cup water
2 tbsp Demerara (raw brown) sugar
2 cloves
1 cinnamon stick (about 4 cm/1½ in)
1 bay leaf

Corn bread (see p.178)

method

Soak the beans overnight. Drain, place in a heavy 4-litre soup pan, cover with 2.2 litres/4 pints of water, bring to a boil, and boil vigorously for 10 minutes, regularly skimming the foam that rises to the surface. Add the onion, garlic and bay leaves. Reduce the heat, partly cover, and simmer for 1 hour 30 minutes.

Prepare the marinated onions. Place the red onion in a bowl and sprinkle with a large pinch of salt. Add the grated zest from ½ the orange, the juice from the orange and the sliced chilli. Set aside. Place the cider vinegar, water, sugar and spices in a non-reactive saucepan, bring to a boil, and simmer for 5 minutes. Pour the hot vinegar over the onions, and leave to cool and infuse while the soup is cooking. You can also make them the day before. These onions will keep refrigerated for a week.

Preheat the oven to 180°C/350°F/Gas Mark 4.

Peel (see p.142) and quarter the tomatoes. Chop the courgettes and peppers into 1.5 cm/½ in pieces. Place the vegetables and garlic cloves in a roasting dish, sprinkle with the spices, season with salt and freshly ground pepper, and drizzle with oil. Bake for 40 minutes, stirring the vegetables twice during baking.

When ready, add the vegetables and chipotle to the beans, and simmer for 30 minutes. Check the seasoning (salt or more chipotle) and simmer for another 30 minutes.

Meanwhile, cook the corn bread (see p.178). Serve the soup with warm corn bread and the marinated red onions.

tip

Always cook your beans thoroughly. Start by boiling them vigorously for 10 minutes to eliminate a toxin called lectin, which is found in raw beans and which can cause gastric problems and food poisoning.

Prawn & crab gumbo

Serves 6 (half the recipe
will make a starter for 4)
Preparation: 25 minutes
+ time to make the stock
Cooking time: 45 minutes

Gumbo is a speciality of Louisiana, USA. It is a thick soup made with seafood and okra. There are as many gumbo recipes as cooks, but you won't have the full gumbo experience without '*filé*' powder. *Filé* is made from crushed sassafras leaves, which are indigenous to the area. The powder is added at the end and should not be boiled. Unfortunately, it is hard to find *filé*, but you can order it online. Otherwise, use arrowroot mixed with fresh thyme leaves.

ingredients

3 tbsp olive oil

2 onions, peeled and finely chopped

2 red (bell) peppers, deseeded and
  finely chopped

2 green (bell) peppers, deseeded and
  finely chopped

2 celery sticks with leaves, finely
  chopped

Salt and pepper

6 garlic cloves, crushed

1 tbsp fresh oregano, chopped

2 tsp ground cumin

2 tsp paprika

1 tbsp hot sauce (such as Tabasco)

1.5 litres/2¾ pints chicken or
  fish stock

400 g/14 oz okra, tailed and sliced

24 king prawn (jumbo shrimp) tails
  (450 g/1 lb), shelled

1 to 2 tbsp *filé* powder (optional), or
  4 tbsp arrowroot mixed with
  3 tbsp water and 2 tsp crushed
  fresh thyme leaves

300 g/11 oz fresh crab meat

250 g/9 oz/1¼ cups basmati rice,
  cooked, to serve

method

Heat the oil in a 4-litre soup pan. Add the onions, peppers and celery, and fry over medium heat for 10 minutes, until soft and lightly caramelized. Season halfway through. Add the crushed garlic, oregano, spices and hot sauce, and cook, stirring, for 1 more minute. Add the chicken or fish stock. Bring to a boil, and simmer for 20 minutes.

Meanwhile, cook the rice in boiling water for 8 minutes. Drain, return to the pan, and leave over very low heat (use a heat diffuser if needed) until the soup is ready.

Add the okra and cook for 10 minutes. Add the prawns and bring to a simmer. If using the arrowrrot and thyme paste, add it now and let it boil for 1 minute. Stir well until it thickens. If using gumbo *filé*, turn off the heat and gradually add the *filé* powder until it thickens. The soup is ready.

Serve with crab meat, rice and extra hot sauce on the side.

❝ No crab? Gumbo also loves leftover fish, chicken or sausages. ❞

stocks & extras

This chapter contains all the bits and pieces you will need for your soups: stocks, dumplings, croutons, and other accompaniments.

Stocks are the most important ingredient for soups. Basic chicken, beef, pork and fish stocks are, of course, present, along with three different recipes for vegetable stocks to give your vegetable soups their own identity.

There is also a section on dumplings, which opens the door to a whole new menu of soup creation. The traditional wonton recipe comes from the mouth of a Chinese cook. The secret of the light and airy liver dumplings lies in the use of brioche. The flavour of the potato dumplings, or, as they're known in Austria, *knödel*, comes from baking the potatoes rather than boiling them. And the matzo balls recipe was given to me by an amazing Jewish cook. I have also included crêpe dumplings, which are not French but an Austrian classic.

No soup book would be complete without bread recipes. The hazelnut and beer wholemeal bread has a beautiful light texture and really crispy crust. The rye and caraway soda bread and the corn bread are both quick and easy to make. I have also included a detailed recipe on how to make the best croutons. The soup recipes will indicate which of these breads will make the most appropriate accompaniment.

stocks

Chicken stock

Makes 1.5 litres/2¾ pints
(for 2.5 litres/4½ pints, double
the ingredients and use
3 litres/5¼ pints of water)
Preparation: 10 minutes
Cooking time: 2 hours

ingredients
1 kg/2¼ lb chicken wings
1 onion, peeled and
cut into 6 wedges
1 large carrot, washed and
cut into chunks
1 small celery stick, cut into chunks
3 garlic cloves, unpeeled
Salt and freshly ground black pepper
1 bay leaf

There is nothing like homemade chicken stock. Chicken wings are cheap (even free-range ones) and perfect to make stock. I roast them in a hot oven first to really draw out the flavours. This stock is also delicious as a soup served with croutons (see p.172) or dumplings (see p.168).

method
Preheat the oven to 220°C/425°F/Gas Mark 7.

Place the chicken wings, onion, carrots, celery and garlic in a roasting dish and bake for 40 minutes. They should be golden and crisp on the edges. Season well and return to the oven for 5 minutes.

Remove from the oven and place the wings and vegetables in a 3-litre soup pan. Pour the fat into a bowl and use it for cooking. Some of the wings will have stuck to the bottom of the pan. Add about 250 ml/9 fl oz/1 cup of water to the pan, scrape well with a wooden spatula to detach all the bits, and add that liquid to the pot, along with 1.5 litres/2¾ pints of water. Bring to a boil, remove the white foam that forms on the surface, and add the bay leaf. Reduce the heat and simmer, partly covered, for 1 hour. Skim the top from time to time.

Turn off the heat, and leave to cool slightly. Place a sieve over a pan or bowl, and ladle the stock into the sieve. This will prevent any splashing of the hot liquid. Unfortunately, the meat from the wings will have lost all its taste through cooking. (You can still scrape it and add it to the soup for bulk.) Let the stock settle, then remove the fat from the surface, or refrigerate overnight and remove the congealed fat from the surface. This stock will keep for a couple of days in the fridge or for 6 months in the freezer. Write the date on the container.

tip
For a Chinese-style chicken stock, add 4 tsp of sliced ginger, 5 chopped spring onions (scallions) and 100 ml/3½ fl oz/scant ½ cup of rice wine to your simmering stock.

Carcass chicken stock

Makes 1.3 litres/2¼ pints
Preparation: 10 minutes
Cooking time: 1 hour

Keep the carcass from a roast chicken, turkey, partridge or duck.
You can freeze carcasses and use them whenever you have time to make
a stock. It will be ready in half the time of a traditional stock.

ingredients

500 g/1 lb 2 oz chicken carcass
1 onion, roughly chopped
1 carrot, scrubbed and roughly chopped
1 small celery stick, roughly chopped
3 garlic cloves
1 organic chicken stock cube
1.5 litres/2¾ pints water
Salt and pepper

method

Place all the ingredients in a 3-litre soup pan. Bring to a boil, reduce the heat
and simmer, mostly covered, for 1 hour. Season to taste. Pass through a sieve
using the same technique as for chicken stock (p.154).

Keep it in the fridge for a couple of days or in the freezer for 6 months.
Write the date on the container.

Beef stock

Makes 2 litres/3½ pints
Preparation: 10 minutes
Cooking time: 2 hours 15 minutes

There are different ways to make beef stock. My favourite one is made from oxtail. It is the same method as for chicken stock: the meat is first roasted in the oven to get the best flavour and also to remove some of the fat. If you make the stock a day ahead, you can easily skim off all the fat from the surface. Scrape the meat off the bone and use in soups or in a salad with shallots, parsley and gherkins.

ingredients
1.25 kg/2¾ lb oxtail
1 onion, chopped
1 carrot, scrubbed and chopped
1 celery stick, chopped
4 garlic cloves, unpeeled
1 leek, washed well
and roughly sliced
2 star anise
Salt and pepper
1 bay leaf

tip
Two ways to remove the fat from the stock: place the pan in cold water first, then in iced water, and remove the fat on the surface, or place in the fridge overnight then remove the fat that has congealed on the surface.

method
Preheat the oven to 220°C/425°F/Gas Mark 7.

Place the oxtail pieces, onion, carrot, celery and garlic in a roasting dish and bake for 35 minutes. Add the leek and star anise and season well. Bake for another 10 minutes.

Remove from the oven. Place the oxtail pieces, vegetables, star anise and bay leaf in a 4-litre soup pan. Pour the fat into a bowl and reserve it for cooking. Add 250 ml/9 fl oz/1 cup of boiling water from the kettle to the pan, and scrape any bits that have stuck to the bottom. Pour the liquid into the pot. Add 2 litres/3½ pints of hot water, bring to a boil, and skim any foam and fat at the surface. Reduce the heat and simmer, mostly covered, for 1½ hours. Skim the surface from time to time.

Turn off the heat, and let it cool down for 15 minutes. Place a sieve over a pan or bowl, and ladle the stock into the sieve. This will prevent any splashing of the hot liquid.

Remove the fat from the surface (see tip), then use. It will keep in the fridge for a couple of days or in the freezer for 6 months. Write the date on the container.

Vegetable stocks

You will have noticed that I like to do a specific stock for each soup, and I will often simmer the peels from the vegetables I use in the recipe to make the stock. I strongly believe that when it comes to soups, one vegetable stock to fit all is too boring, especially if you are vegetarian. In the same way we use chicken, beef or pork stock to achieve different flavours, I have given each of the following stocks a very specific identity.

Brown vegetable stock

Makes 1.3 litres/2¼ pints
Preparation: 10 minutes
Cooking time: 45 minutes

An earthy stock to use with mushrooms, beetroot, black beans and lentils.

ingredients

10 g/¼ oz dried porcini mushrooms
3 tbsp olive oil
100 g/3½ oz shallots, chopped
100 g/3½ oz carrots, scrubbed
   and chopped
250 g/9 oz assorted mushrooms,
   chopped

Salt and pepper
2 garlic cloves, peeled and
   roughly chopped
1 tsp tomato paste
1 tsp coriander seeds
A few fresh thyme sprigs

tip
For 2 litres/3½ pints of stock:
use 1½ quantity of ingredients
and 2 litres/3½ pints of water.

method

Soak the dried mushrooms in 200 ml/7 fl oz of warm water for 15 minutes.

Meanwhile, prepare the ingredients. Heat the oil in a 3-litre soup pan. Add the shallots and carrots, and cook over medium heat for 5 minutes. Raise the heat to high, add the chopped fresh mushrooms and stir-fry for 5 minutes, until the mushrooms are soft.

Season well with salt and plenty of freshly ground black pepper and cook for another 3 to 4 minutes, until most of the moisture has evaporated. Add the garlic, tomato paste and coriander seeds and cook for a minute. Add the soaked dried mushrooms, their soaking water and 1.3 litres/2¼ pints fresh water and bring to a simmer. Skim the foam off the surface, add the thyme and simmer for 30 minutes.

Pass through a sieve using the same technique as before. It will keep for 3 days in the fridge or in the freezer for 6 months. Write the date on the container.

Green vegetable stock

Makes 1.3 litres/2¼ pints
Preparation: 10 minutes
Cooking time: 40 minutes

A light stock to use with root vegetables, leeks and spinach.

ingredients

2 tbsp olive oil

100 g/3½ oz onions, cubed

100 g/3½ oz leeks, washed well
    and sliced

100 g/3½ oz fennel, cubed

100 g/3½ oz carrots, scrubbed
    and cubed

1 small celery stick, chopped

Salt and pepper

15 g/½ oz parsley sprigs

method

Heat the oil in a 3-litre soup pan. Add the vegetables and cook over medium heat for 5 minutes until soft. Season well with salt and pepper and cook for another 5 minutes, until slightly caramelized. The salt will draw moisture and extra flavour out of the vegetables.

Add 1.5 litres/2¾ pints of water, bring to a simmer, add the parsley, and cook, mostly covered, for 30 minutes. Pass through a sieve using the same technique as before. It will keep for 3 days in the fridge or in the freezer for 6 months.

tip

For 2 litres/3½ pints of stock: use 1½ quantity of ingredients and 2.2 litres/3¾ pints of water.

For 2.2 litres/3¾ pints of stock: double the quantity of ingredients and use 2.7 litres/4¾ pints of water.

Red vegetable stock

Makes 1.3 litres/2¼ pints
Preparation: 10 minutes
Cooking time: 40 minutes

Moorish intense stock to use with tomato, pumpkin and aubergine.

ingredients

2 tbsp olive oil

150 g/5 oz onion, cubed

200 g/7 oz tomatoes,
    roughly chopped

125 g/4 oz red (bell) pepper,
    deseeded and cubed

125 g/4 oz green (bell) pepper,
    deseeded and cubed

Salt

⅛ tsp chilli powder

Pinch of saffron

½ cinnamon stick

3 garlic cloves, unpeeled

method

This is a similar recipe to the previous one. Cook the vegetables for 10 minutes, adding salt halfway through. Then add the spices and garlic, and cook for 1 minute. Double the amount of chilli powder if you want a spicy stock. Cover with 1.5 litres/2¾ pints water, and cook for 30 minutes. Pass through a sieve using the same technique as before. It will keep for 3 days in the fridge or in the freezer for 6 months.

tip

For 2 litres/3½ pints of stock: use 1½ quantity of ingredients and 2.2 litres/3¾ pints of water.

For 2.2 litres/3¾ pints of stock: double the quantity of ingredients and use 2.7 litres/4¾ pints of water.

Fish stock

Makes 1.3 litres/2¼ pints
Preparation: 15 minutes
Cooking time: 25 minutes

Ask your fishmonger to put heads and bones of fish aside for you. This is very cheap and sometimes free. Avoid oily fish, which give a strong, almost bitter, flavour. If you are filleting fish, you can also freeze the heads and bones to use in a future stock. Fish stock should not simmer for too long, or you will lose the fresh taste of fish. If you need to reduce it, sieve it first, then boil it down. Lime leaves can be bought from some Oriental stores frozen and will keep in the freezer forever. They bring a wonderful, clean, zesty flavour to fish stock.

ingredients

1.5 kg/3 lb 6 oz fish heads and bones
3 tbsp cooking olive oil
1 onion, peeled and cubed
200 g/7 oz fennel, washed and cubed
200 g/7 oz carrot, washed and cubed
2 large garlic cloves, peeled and chopped
Salt
150 ml/5 fl oz/⅔ cup white wine
3 frozen lime leaves
12 peppercorns
150 g/5 oz mussels, scrubbed

method

Clean the fish heads and bones. Remove any gills and traces of blood, which would add bitterness. Heat the oil in a 4-litre soup pan because the fish heads take up a lot of space before they cook down. Add the vegetables and cook over low-medium heat for 6–7 minutes, until soft but not caramelized.

Raise the heat to medium, add the fish heads and bones and cook for 10 minutes, or until they lose their smell of raw fish. Stir occasionally, making sure nothing burns at the bottom. Season well with salt. Add the wine and let it reduce for 2 minutes. Add 1.5 litres/2¾ pints of water, bring to a simmer, and skim the foam off the top. Add the lime leaves and peppercorns. Reduce the heat and simmer for 20 minutes. Add the mussels and simmer for 4 more minutes. Turn off the heat and let it sit for 10 minutes. Ladle the stock into a sieve set on a bowl or pot. Use it within 24 hours, or freeze for up to 6 months.

tip

If you want a richer stock, discard the mussel shells, whiz the stock in the blender, then pass it through a fine sieve.

dumplings & croutons

This section opens the door to a whole new soup menu. Any of these dumplings can be served with a simple stock to create a soup.

Chinese wonton

Makes 36 wontons (about
5–6 wontons per serving)
Preparation: 45 minutes
Cooking time: 7 minutes

This traditional Chinese dumpling has a worldwide reputation. Wonton skins or pasta squares can be bought from Chinese and Thai supermarkets. They make lovely melt-in-the-mouth dumplings. They are perfect served in a Chinese-style chicken stock (see tip on p.154).

ingredients

2 tsp dried black mushrooms
125 g/4 oz raw king prawn (jumbo shrimp) tails, peeled
250 g/9 oz minced (ground) pork
50 g/2 oz/¼ cup tinned water chestnuts, roughly chopped
2 tsp grated ginger
1 large spring onion (scallion), or 20 g/¾ oz/2½ tbsp Chinese chives, chopped
1½ tsp toasted sesame oil
20 g/¾ oz celery or fennel, chopped
Salt and freshly ground black pepper
1 tbsp light soy sauce

1 x 200 g/7 oz pack of wonton pastry or skins

method

Place the dried mushrooms in a bowl, cover with boiling water and leave for 10 minutes.

De-vein the prawns. With a sharp knife, make a shallow incision along the spine of each prawn. You will see the vein that lies inside. Lift and pull the vein with the tip of the knife: it should come out easily. These veins are not dangerous to eat, but they can add a gritty, unpleasant taste to the mixture. Press the prawns between two sheets of kitchen roll to extract as much moisture as possible.

Place all the ingredients except the seasoning and soy sauce in a blender. Mix by pulsing a few times. It should be well blended but still have some texture.

Transfer the mixture to a bowl. Season with salt and pepper, then add the soy sauce and mix well.

Hold a wonton skin in your palm. Place a big teaspoonful of the mixture in the centre, dip a finger in water and lightly wet the edges. Fold in half and press the edges together. You will have a rectangle. Wet the two extremities of the rectangle with water, bring together and pinch to seal. Place on a tray and repeat with the others.

You can keep the wontons refrigerated for 24 hours. Cook them in boiling water for 4–5 minutes. Remove with a slotted spoon, drain well, and place into serving bowls. Cover with Chinese-style chicken stock, and garnish with finely sliced spring onions and a drizzle of sesame oil.

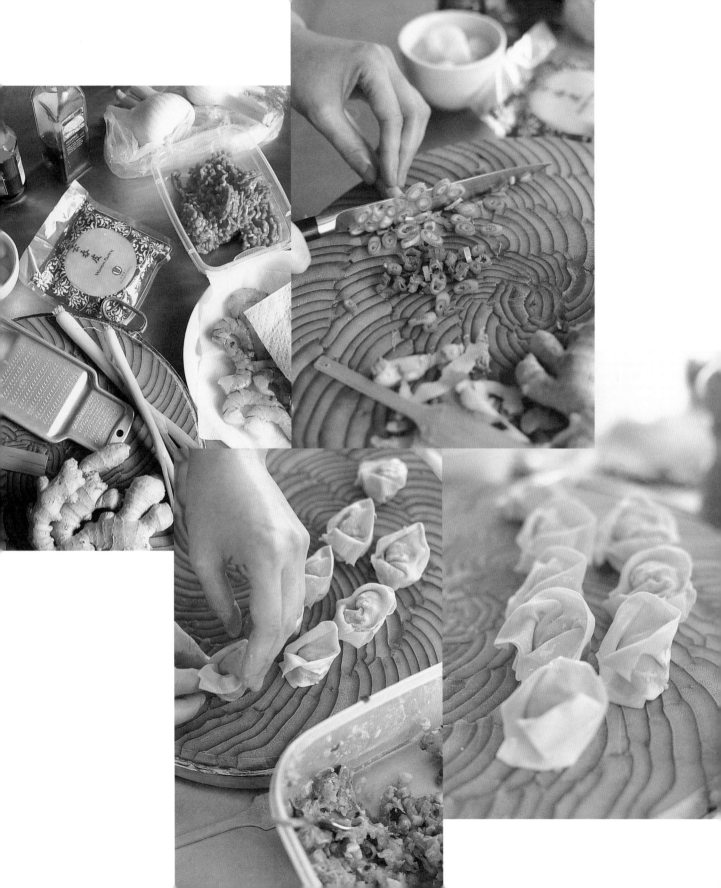

Matzo balls

Makes about 20 balls
Preparation: 10 minutes
+ 1 hour in the fridge
Cooking time: 45 minutes

Matzha is the unleavened bread served during Jewish Passover. The bread is crushed into a meal to make matzo balls, or *knaidlach* in Yiddish (a word derived from *knödel*). They are the traditional dumplings for chicken soup. This recipe was kindly given to me by Mamie Céline, who is famous for her delicious Passover meals.

ingredients

4 eggs
2 tbsp onion, grated
1 tsp parsley, finely chopped
1 tsp salt

Freshly ground black pepper
150 g/5 oz/generous ¾ cup matzo meal
60 ml/2 fl oz/¼ cup oil
120 ml/4 fl oz/½ cup chicken stock

method

Break the eggs into a bowl, and whisk for 2 minutes until fluffy. Add the grated onion, parsley and salt. Season to taste with black pepper and mix well.

In a separate bowl, place the matzo meal, oil and chicken stock. Mix until well blended and smooth. Add the egg mixture and mix vigorously for 2 minutes, until well blended. Place a piece of clingfilm directly on the surface and refrigerate for at least 1 hour.

Place 2.5 litres/2½ pints of water into a 3-litre saucepan and bring to a simmer. Meanwhile, oil or wet your hands. Place a tablespoon of matzo dough in your hand and roll it into a ball. Set aside on a plate while you make the rest.

Add salt to the simmering water and drop the balls into the water. Simmer, gently covered, for 35–40 minutes. The balls are compact and take a long time to cook. They will expand slightly while cooking. Matzo balls are usually cooked in water rather than stock because they absorb a lot of liquid. To serve, reheat in simmering chicken soup and serve with chopped dill.

Austrian liver dumplings

Makes 16 dumplings
Preparation: 20 minutes
Cooking time: 20 minutes

In Austria dumplings go hand in hand with soups. The variety is overwhelming. This liver dumpling is one of my favourites because of its lightness. It goes wonderfully well with the Jabugo consommé (see p.114) and is also delicious in a chicken stock.

ingredients

60 g/2½ oz brioche rolls or slices,
cut into small pieces
100 ml/3½ fl oz/scant ½ cup milk
300 g/11 oz chicken liver
60 g/2½ oz/generous ½ stick butter,
at room temperature
100 g/3½ oz/²⁄₃ cup shallots,
finely chopped
2 large egg yolks
45 g/1½ oz/¹⁄₃ cup dried breadcrumbs
1 tbsp fresh parsley,
roughly chopped
1 tbsp fresh chives, roughly chopped
Salt and pepper

method

Place the brioche pieces in a small bowl, cover with the milk, and set aside.

The chicken liver should be light in colour, plump, firm and shiny. With a sharp knife, remove any stringy, hard centre and traces of blood. Cut into small pieces.

Heat 2 teaspoons of the butter in a small frying pan and cook the shallots for 2–3 minutes, until soft and slightly caramelized. Transfer to a bowl to cool.

Squeeze the brioche to remove most of the moisture, and place in the bowl of a food processor with the chicken liver, egg yolks, breadcrumbs, parsley, chives, cooled shallots and remaining butter. Process with just a few pulses. It should be well blended with some texture. Transfer to a bowl and season well with salt and freshly ground black pepper. If you don't have a food processor, finely chop the chicken liver and mix all the ingredients in a bowl, squeezing them between your fingers.

Place in the fridge for 30 minutes.

When ready, bring a saucepan of water to a simmer. Using two spoons, form little egg-shaped dumplings of about a large tablespoon each, and drop them into the simmering water. Simmer for 7–8 minutes, and lift them out of the water with a slotted spoon. Let them drain for a few seconds and place in the soup pan or the soup bowls. Cook them in 2 batches.

Potato *knödel*

Makes about 24 *knödel*
Preparation: 1 hour 5 minutes
+ 1 hour cooling time
Cooking time: 5 minutes

Knödel are the Austrian cousins of *gnocchi*. They are served with the Goulash soup (p.132). I have baked the potatoes because it accentuates the potato flavour in the dumplings. It will also give the dough a dryer texture, so it needs less flour, and the result is a lighter dumpling.

ingredients
500 g/1 lb 2 oz baking potatoes
60 g/2½ oz/generous ½ stick butter
1 egg + 1 egg yolk
50 g/2 oz/⅓ cup plain (all-purpose) flour
50 g/2 oz/⅓ cup cornflour (cornstarch)
¼ tsp freshly grated nutmeg
Salt and pepper

method
Preheat the oven to 200°C/400°F/Gas Mark 6. Place the potatoes on a baking tray and bake for 1 hour.

When cool enough to handle but still warm, peel the potatoes and mash them with the butter. Add the whole egg and egg yolk, the two flours, the nutmeg, and seasoning. Mix well and quickly. Leave to cool in the fridge for 1 hour. Roll into little balls and poach in simmering water for 4–5 minutes.

tip
Best made on the day.

" Lighter when just cooked; eat them straight away if you can. "

Chive crêpe dumplings

Makes about 8 crêpes
Preparation: 10 minutes
+ 20 minutes to rest the batter
Cooking time: 20 minutes

You might imagine a large crêpe floating on your soup, but in fact the crêpes are rolled and cut into thin noodle-like strips. It is not a French invention but yet another Austrian one. They are best made at the last minute, but the batter can be mixed the day before. They can also be served rolled on the side.

ingredients

50 g/2 oz/½ stick butter
125 g/4 oz/generous ¾ cup plain (all-purpose) flour
¼ tsp salt
¼ tsp freshly grated nutmeg
Freshly ground black pepper
1 large egg
1 large egg yolk
250 ml/9 fl oz/1 cup milk
1 tbsp fresh chives, finely chopped

25 g/1 oz/¼ stick butter, for cooking the crêpes, melted

method

Make the golden butter. Place the butter into a small saucepan over a very low heat. Let it warm for about 10 minutes until it becomes golden (if you use a stainless steel or white enamel saucepan, it's easier to check the colour). Do not let it burn. Transfer the butter immediately to a bowl.

Meanwhile, mix the flour, salt, nutmeg and pepper. Add the eggs and egg yolk and slowly whisk in the milk. Add the chives and golden butter and give it a final stir. Don't overwork the dough: it's fine if some lumps remain. Cover the bowl with clingfilm and leave to rest for 20 minutes.

Heat a 25 cm/10 in non-stick frying pan. Brush the pan with butter. Pour about 80 ml/3 fl oz/⅓ cup of batter into the pan and swirl it around quickly to coat the pan. Cook for 1 minute. Flip the crêpe over with a spatula and cook the other side for 1 minute. Slide onto a plate, roll, and keep covered while you make the other crêpes.

Finely slice the rolled crêpes, place the thin strips in each bowl, and cover with hot soup or stock.

Croutons

Makes 4-6 servings
Preparation: 5 minutes
Cooking time: 5 minutes

ingredients
150 g/5 oz slightly dry bread
50 g/2 oz/½ stick butter, cut into small pieces
2 tbsp olive oil
Sea salt and freshly ground pepper

tip
Add crushed garlic or spices when the butter is still foaming, cook for 30 seconds, then add the croutons.

Like the perfect fried egg, it is an art to make perfect croutons. They should be light and crispy and not overloaded with fat. The quality of your frying pan is crucial. A heavy, thick frying pan will keep an even temperature. Thinner pans will tend to warm up or cool down too quickly. The second crucial element is the temperature of the fat. If it is too high, the bread will burn; if it is too low, the bread will absorb too much fat and the croutons will be heavy. Any bread is good for croutons, but it is best if it is a couple of days old. To cook evenly, the cubes of bread should be of similar size. You will find a recipe for saffron brioche croutons on p.123.

method
Cut the bread into even cubes.

Heat the butter and oil in a heavy frying pan. When the butter stops foaming, add the croutons. Stir and toss the croutons until well browned on all sides. This will take 2–3 minutes. Place on a warm plate and sprinkle lightly with salt and freshly ground pepper. Toss well and use while still warm.

Toasted garlic breadcrumbs

Makes 4-6 servings
Preparation: 10 minutes
Cooking: 25 minutes

ingredients
150 g/5 oz slightly dry bread
3 tbsp duck fat (see p.136), or olive oil
2 large garlic cloves
Salt and pepper

This is an alternative to croutons that works really well in chunky soups like the Bean and duck confit (p.136). The breadcrumbs will taste better if they are dry.

method
Preheat the oven to 180°C/150°F/Gas Mark 4.

To make dry breadcrumbs, remove the crusts from the bread, cut into chunks, place in the food processor and blend until you get crumbs. Spread the crumbs onto a baking tray and bake for 15–20 minutes, until dry but not brown. You should obtain about 100 g/3½ oz/2 cups of dried breadcrumbs.

Heat the duck fat over a medium heat in a large frying pan. Add the garlic and cook for 30 seconds, until it sizzles but before it browns. Add the breadcrumbs and pan-fry for 2–3 minutes, until crisp and golden. Transfer to a serving bowl and set aside.

breads

You can't have a soup book without a few bread recipes. In addition to the traditional wholemeal or yeast-free breads, I have included *pirojkis* and *gougères*, which make unusual and delicious accompaniments to soups.

Hazelnut & beer bread

Makes 1 loaf
Preparation: 35 minutes
Cooking time: 40 minutes

ingredients

200 ml/7 fl oz/generous ¾ cup lager
beer
150 ml/5 fl oz/⅔ cup water
1 tsp dried yeast
500 g/1 lb 2 oz/3⅓ cups wholemeal
(whole-wheat) bread flour
100 g/3½ oz/⅔ cup toasted and
chopped hazelnuts
1½ tsp salt
1 tsp sugar

I like the flavour beer gives to bread. In addition to making it lighter, without using too much yeast, it creates a delicious crispy crust.

method

Pour the beer and water into a bowl and place over a pan of simmering water to warm up the beer slightly. It should be slightly warmer than your hand. Add the yeast. Stir with a fork to dissolve the yeast. Leave the mixture for 15 minutes until bubbly on the surface.

Mix the flour, hazelnuts, salt and sugar.

Make a well in the centre of the flour. Add the beer mixture and mix until well blended. Work the dough for 2–3 minutes, then leave to rest for 10 minutes. This will give time for the flour to absorb all the moisture. Knead the dough on the work surface for at least 10 minutes, ideally 15 minutes. To check that your dough is ready, tear a small piece out and slowly stretch it. If it pulls easily and the light comes through, it is ready.

Roll the dough into a ball. Place in a large bowl. Cover loosely with clingfilm and let it rise for 2–2½ hours.

Punch the dough to reduce the volume and place it on the kitchen counter. Don't knead it again. Slightly flatten the dough and roll the edges inwards towards the centre, giving the dough a quarter of a turn each time. Turn the dough over. Hold the dough between your hands, slowly turn it on itself to really shape it into a ball. Place on a piece of baking paper, make a few cuts on top, and leave to rise for 40 minutes. Meanwhile, preheat the oven to 220°C/425°F/ Gas Mark 7. Leave a baking tray in the oven.

Lift the bread with the paper and place on the hot baking tray inside the oven. Bake for 20 minutes, then lower the heat to 190°C/375°F/Gas Mark 5 and bake for another 20 minutes. To make sure it is cooked, tap the bottom of the bread. It should sound hollow. Take out of the oven and leave to cool. Serve when it is just slightly warm.

Rye soda bread
with caraway seeds

Makes 4 servings
Preparation: 45 minutes
Cooking time: 45 minutes

Soda bread is a well-known yeast-free Irish bread made with bicarbonate of soda. I have adapted the recipe to a rye and caraway bread that will go beautifully with the Black Beluga lentil soup (p.115) and Borscht (p.144). My friend Barbara, who is a wonderful baker, doesn't use buttermilk in her soda bread because she finds it expensive and hard to get hold of. She mixes milk with lemon juice and leaves the mixture to curdle and sour. I have used her trick in this recipe.

ingredients

350 ml/12 fl oz/1½ cups milk
Juice of ½ lemon
350 g/12 oz/2⅓ cups wholemeal (whole-wheat) rye flour
150 g/5 oz/1 cup plain (all-purpose) flour
1½ tsp bicarbonate of soda
2 tbsp cocoa powder (unsweetened cocoa)
¾ tsp salt
1½ tsp caraway seeds
1 tbsp molasses sugar

method

Preheat the oven to 220°C/425°F/Gas Mark 7.

Mix the milk and lemon juice and leave for 30 minutes.

Mix the rye flour, plain flour, bicarbonate of soda, cocoa and salt. Sift into a large bowl. Add 1 teaspoon caraway seeds. Warm up 100 ml/3½ fl oz/scant ½ cup of the sour milk in a small saucepan and dissolve the molasses sugar in it.

Make a well in the centre of the flour mixture. Pour in the sweet, warm milk and most of the sour milk. Mix in gradually until you obtain a soft, sticky dough. You might not need all of the sour milk.

Gather the dough and place in a lightly oiled 900 g/2 lb cake tin. Mark a deep line on the top with a knife and sprinkle with the remaining caraway seeds. Place in the oven and bake for 10 minutes. Reduce the oven temperature to 200°C/400°F/Gas Mark 6 and bake for 35 minutes.

Leave to cool, or it will be difficult to slice and serve.

Corn bread

Makes 8 slices
Preparation: 15 minutes
Cooking time: 25 minutes

Corn bread is one of my husband Rawdon's specialities, to the point where I rarely make it and he always does. He makes a wonderful turkey stuffing out of this bread with loads of chopped onions and celery and moistened with a good homemade chicken stock. Corn bread is an ideal last-minute bread to accompany any soup, but it goes really well with Black bean soup (p.148).

ingredients

200 g/7 oz/scant 1¼ cups coarse cornmeal or polenta
100 g/3½ oz/⅔ cup plain (all-purpose) flour
1 tsp sugar
½ tsp salt
2½ tsp baking powder
250 ml/9 fl oz/1 cup milk
1 large egg
85 g/3 oz/¾ stick butter

tip

You can add fried bacon bits, fried onion, cheese or chilli to the batter to vary the taste.

method

Preheat the oven to 220°C/425°F/Gas Mark 7.

Mix the cornmeal or polenta, the flour, sugar, salt and baking powder. Sift into a bowl.

In a separate bowl, lightly whisk together the milk and egg.

Put 25 g/1 oz/5 tsp of the butter into a heavy skillet or a round baking tray, and place this in the oven for 3 minutes, spreading it around the pan halfway through. Meanwhile, melt the rest of the butter in a small saucepan, mix it into the milk and egg mixture and add to the flour mixture. Mix quickly until well blended, but do not overwork the batter. Take the skillet out of the oven and pour in the cornmeal mixture. Return to the oven, reduce the heat to 200°C/400°F/Gas Mark 6, and bake for about 20–25 minutes.

There are two ways to check that the cornmeal is ready: it should detach slightly from the edges, and when you prick the centre of the cake with a toothpick, it should come out clean.

Leave to cool slightly, then cut into slices or squares, and serve while still warm.

Pirojki dough

Makes 18 *pirojkis*
Preparation: 45 minutes
Proving time: 2 hours

Pirojkis are a Russian speciality. They are small savoury pastries eaten as snacks or traditionally served with Borscht (p.144). *Pirojkis* can be made with shortcrust or puff pastry. My favourite ones melt in the mouth and are made with this light brioche-like dough.

ingredients

125 ml/4 fl oz/½ cup milk
1½ tsp dried yeast
¼ tsp sugar
320 g/11½ oz/generous 2 cups
strong white bread flour
¾ tsp salt
3 eggs
50 g/2 oz/½ stick butter, softened

method

Pour the milk into a bowl and place over a pan of simmering water to warm up the milk. It should be slightly warmer than your hand. Dilute the yeast in the milk. Add the sugar, and leave aside for 15 minutes until foamy and bubbly on top.

In a large bowl, mix the flour and salt. In a separate bowl, mix one egg and two egg yolks. Make a well in the centre of the flour. Add the milk mixture and the eggs. Mix until well blended. The mixture should be dry and compact, not soft or runny. Leave it for 15 minutes. Place the dough on the counter top and flatten slightly. Place the soft butter in the centre, fold the edges over the butter to enclose it. Start kneading the dough to incorporate the butter. Continue kneading for 10–15 minutes, until elastic. Roll into a ball and leave to rest in a lightly oily bowl, covered, for 2 hours.

Use the dough straight away, or keep in the fridge, covered, until the next day.

Go to p.144 for instructions on how to make up the Pirojkis.

> *You can make endless combinations of fillings for* pirojkis. *Try mushroom and bacon, cooked potatoes and cheese, or cooked beef and onions.*

Parmesan *gougères*

Makes 18 puffs
Preparation: 15 minutes
Cooking time: 25 minutes

Gougères is the French name for savoury chou puffs. They make a perfect last-minute accompaniment for soup. I sprinkle them with Parmesan cheese, but you can use any hard cheese. There is a trick to keeping them dry and crisp at the end of the baking. You need to let some of the steam gradually escape from the oven but without opening the oven door: keep the door slightly ajar with the handle of a wooden spoon.

ingredients

125 ml/4 fl oz/½ cup milk
125 ml/4 fl oz/½ cup water
110 g/3½ oz/scant 1 stick butter
Salt and pepper
135 g/4½ oz/scant 1 cup plain (all-purpose) flour
4 eggs, lightly beaten
85 g/3 oz/¾ cup Parmesan cheese, finely grated

method

Preheat the oven to 220°C/425°F/Gas Mark 7. Line a large baking tray with baking parchment.

Place the milk, water and butter in a saucepan. Season with a large pinch of salt and freshly ground black pepper and bring to a simmer.

Add the flour and stir quickly. The mixture will naturally form into a ball. Stir over the heat for about a minute, to 'dry' the dough. Transfer into a bowl and add the eggs, a couple of tablespoons at a time, and incorporate, stirring constantly with a wooden spoon.

You can spoon the mixture onto baking parchment, but it's easier to use a piping bag and to pipe 1.5 x 7 cm/½ x 3 in strips. Sprinkle about 2 teaspoons of grated Parmesan over each puff, and bake them for 10 minutes. Reduce the heat to 200°C/400°F/Gas Mark 6, and bake for another 10 to 12 minutes. They should be golden and puffed up.

Turn off the oven, open the oven door very slightly, and place a wooden spoon in the gap to keep the door ajar. Leave for 15 minutes, then serve while still warm. The puffs can be baked in advance and reheated, but they are much better freshly baked.

pastes & mayonnaise

Some of the quick soup recipes use store-bought pastes,
but I have included recipes for delicious
homemade ones here.

Red curry paste

Makes 10 tablespoons of paste
Preparation: 20 minutes

Ready-made pastes are better purchased from specialist Thai stores than from supermarkets, though I do prefer a homemade one. Red curry paste is really simple to make: just chuck all the ingredients in a food processor. When you cook with it, you will really get the flavours from all the individual components coming through.

ingredients

10 dried long chillies
10 fresh green peppercorns
or black peppercorns
½ tsp coarse sea salt
1 tbsp galangal, grated
2 tbsp lemongrass, finely chopped
100 g/3½ oz/⅔ cup shallots, chopped
Cloves of 1 head of garlic, crushed
2 tsp shrimp paste
Grated zest of 1 lime
1 tbsp ground coriander
2 tsp ground cumin seeds

method

Place the chillies in a bowl and cover with boiling water from the kettle. Soak them while you prepare the rest of the ingredients.

Place all the ingredients in a food processor except the chillies and spices. Refresh the chillies under cold water and squeeze dry. Add them to the food processor. Process until blended, pushing down the coarse bits that have stuck to the edges of the bowl. You might have to blend for 3–4 minutes. When the mixture is smooth enough, transfer to a bowl and add the ground coriander and cumin seeds. Stir until well blended.

Spoon into an airtight container and place a piece of clingfilm directly over the surface. The mixture will keep for 2 weeks in the fridge. It doesn't freeze well.

66 Use this paste in the soup recipes or any of your favourite Thai red curries. 99

Aïoli

Makes 6–8 servings
Preparation: 15 minutes

Aïoli is a garlic mayonnaise made without mustard, vinegar or lemon juice.
It is, of course, for garlic lovers, and is one of the best accompaniments for fish soups. The best way to make it is in a pestle and mortar because the garlic has to be crushed into a light paste. I make aïoli with a mixture of grapeseed and olive oils because I find it too heavy with only olive oil. You need a good light olive oil for this, as extra-virgin will be too intense.

ingredients

3–4 large garlic cloves
3 pinches of salt
2 large egg yolks
Freshly ground peppercorn
150 ml/5 fl oz/⅔ cup grapeseed oil
150 ml/5 fl oz/⅔ cup olive oil

tip

If you don't own a pestle and mortar, use a garlic press to crush the cloves, then the back of a spoon to mash them and turn them into a fine paste.

method

It is very important that all the ingredients are at room temperature. Peel the garlic cloves and cut them in half. Remove any green germ from the middle of the cloves: it is bitter and difficult to digest.

Place the garlic and a pinch of salt into a pestle and mortar and crush until you obtain a paste. This might take up to 5 minutes. Add the egg yolks, more salt, and the pepper, and mix well. Season well because once the oil is incorporated, the salt will not blend in much. Leave for 3–4 minutes for the salt and garlic to diffuse into the egg yolks and slightly 'cook' them; it will help the aïoli to be more stable and not separate.

Slowly add the oil, starting with grapeseed oil, a teaspoon at a time at the beginning, whisking the oil into the egg mixture until well blended, finishing off with 3–4 vigorous strokes. As you incorporate the oil, you will feel the mixture thickening. Whisk well before adding any more oil. Finish by adding the olive oil in the same way. You might not need all the oil. Taste the mixture as you go.

for a saffron aïoli

Add a large pinch of saffron, a pinch of turmeric and a pinch of chilli to the egg yolk and garlic and proceed as above, using just 300 ml/½ pint of only grapeseed oil.

Harissa

Makes about 8 tablespoons
of paste
Preparation: 25 minutes
+ 1 hour to cool

Harissa is a chilli and garlic paste from North Africa. The recipe varies slightly from Morocco to Tunisia. Some of my friends cannot eat without a tablespoon of harissa on their plate. They claim it brings out the flavour of every dish. The truth is, harissa is addictive, even more so when it is homemade, so be prepared to be hooked!

ingredients
2 Ramiro red peppers
(about 100 g/3½ oz)
100 g/3½ oz red chillies
(medium-strength, such
as red jalapeños)
4 garlic cloves
1 tsp chilli powder
1 tsp coriander seeds, toasted
and crushed
1 tsp ground cumin
Salt
2 tbsp olive oil

method
Preheat the grill to maximum. Place the peppers and chillies on a baking tray and grill for 10–15 minutes, turning them frequently until all sides are brown. Remove from the oven. The chillies will brown quicker, so you may need to remove them first. Place the peppers and chillies in a bowl and cover with clingfilm. Leave to cool.

When cool enough to handle, remove the skins and seeds from the red peppers. Remove the skins from the chillies but keep the seeds. Place the peeled chillies and peppers in a food processor with the garlic, chilli powder, coriander seeds and cumin, and process until smooth. Season well with salt and process again. Add the olive oil, and process one last time. Transfer to an airtight container, cover the surface with clingfilm, and keep in the fridge for up to 1 month.

Index

Acknowledgements

First published in the United Kingdom in 2010 by
PAVILION BOOKS
10 Southcombe Street, London W14 0RA

An imprint of Anova Books Company Ltd

Text © Valerie Berry, 2010
Design and layout © Anova Books, 2010
Photography © Yuki Sugiura, 2010

The moral right of the author has been asserted.

Commissioning Editor: Emily Preece-Morrison
Photographer: Yuki Sugiura
Food Stylist: Valerie Berry
Prop Stylist: Wei Tang
Concept & Cover Design: Georgina Hewitt
Layout: Anna Pow
Proofreader: Caroline Curtis
Production: Oliver Jeffreys
Index: Patricia Hymans

ISBN: 978-1-86205-897-2

A CIP catalogue record for this book is available from the British Library.

10 9 8 7 6 5 4 3 2 1

Reproduction by Rival Colour Limited, UK
Printed and bound by 1010 International Printing Ltd, China

www.anovabooks.com

Writing the acknowledgments for this book is overwhelming and brings tears to my eyes. I've never worked on a project that has drawn so much enthusiasm and energy from everybody.

My first enormous thank you goes to Wei and Yuki who have put so much of themselves into this book. They have worked like Trojans and done everything possible to make things happen. They have given the book its style and soul.

Thank you to Adrian for welcoming us in his home, letting us photograph his Mercedes and modelling like a pro.

Thanks to Emily for trusting us, giving us the freedom to express ourselves, and for modelling on the beach in the cold.

Thank you to Sophie and Lucy for putting up with yet another of my mad projects and having to get up early to gather clams. They modelled in my first book when they were younger. It was wonderful to have them again and I wish they could be in all my books. Thank you also to their mom Debbie for being so supportive and so enthusiastic about modelling for most of the day. Thank you also to their granddad Peter, the fisherman, who cheerfully ate his soup 47 times while being photographed. Thanks also to his wife Pam for letting us steal him.

Thank you to Karl for letting use his beach hut. Its holiday mood made us feel very relaxed.

Thank you to Rumina and Simon for sharing their home and its treasures and for keeping a brave smiling face while we brought chaos. The book would not be the same without them.

Thank you to Caroline for giving us *carte blanche* in her flat. I regret that she could not be there that day but she was present in spirit and through her inspiring bric-a-brac. Thank you to Dan for entertaining us and bravely accepting to have his knee photographed.

Thank you to Lars for the privilege of using his studio and the stunning furniture he expertly makes. Thanks to him also for playing model so patiently when he had tons of other things to do.

Thank you to Barbara for opening her house and her painter's studio. She made us feel right at home and we will always cherish the memory of that day. I wish we had more time to enjoy the painting lesson.

Thank you to Carine, Matthias and Carlo for playing family dinner and enjoying the whole experience so much. A special thank to Carlo who at 2 years old was the big star of the evening and won all the women's hearts.

Thank you to Mamie Céline for sharing the secret of her Matzo ball recipe and taking the time to hand-write it and describe it beautifully.

Thank you to Barry for giving me 5 litres of gorgeous family-produced olive oil from Crete which played a great part in the recipe testing.

Thank you to Pierre who badly timed his visit to London and ended up washing dishes and testing soup for many days.

Thank you to Aya, Raquel, Linda, Rawdon, and Lars for assisting Yuki and I. They were vital support. Thank you also to Linda for modelling.

Thank you to Rachel, Sue and the residents of Jacqueline House for testing the soups and giving me such wonderful feedback.

Thank you to Rawdon for eating soups all summer long and putting up with my obsessive testing; for having ants crawl up his legs while modelling; for having to wear clothes three sizes too small; for doing his back in while moving equipment on location, but above all, a huge thank you for his constant uplifting enthusiasm.

A special thought to Emma, Dan and little Evie who couldn't be in the photographs because a few days before Evie badly broke her leg.

This book comes from the heart of everyone who has had a role in it.